How to Sell Millions of Your Product on TV and in Retail:

Learn the Secrets Behind the OxiClean Success & How You Can Follow the Same Model

By Jon LaClare

Copyright 2011 Jon LaClare

ISBN 978-1-4357-9119-0

Paperback ISBN: 978-1-257-65214-3

Table of Contents

Introduction: As Seen on TV… Your Product! vii
Chapter 1: The OxiClean Story—From a Humble Garage to a $325million Payday 1
Chapter 2: How to Make Millions— 7 Steps to Turning Products into Profits 7
Chapter 3: The 7 Laws of the Harvest... 17
Chapter 4: 10 Steps for Producing Infomercials That Sell................ 25
Chapter 5: TV to Retail—The REAL Road to Riches 35
Chapter 6: Don't Forget About HSN/QVC (Hey, A Little More Revenue Never Hurt Anyone!)....................................... 41
Chapter 7: How to Manage Your Business So It Runs Itself......... 45
Chapter 8: With a Great Idea, You Don't Need Money................ 49
Chapter 9: Free Advertising! How Even Billion Dollar Brands Are Starting to Use Infomercial Marketing................. 51
Chapter 10: Increase Your Odds of Success with Market Research 55
Chapter 11: Test, Test, Test 61
Chapter 12: Patents, Trademarks and Contract Review.................. 69
Chapter 13: The History of Infomercials, Or: Growing from the Basement to the Penthouse 75
Chapter 14: Example Financial Projections for a Successful Launch 81
Chapter 15: Does the Snuggie Come in Yellow? (And Other Frequently Asked Questions) 85
Chapter 16: Industry Resources—The Best of the Best................... 91
About the Author 97

Introduction

As Seen on TV… __Your__ Product!

The Pet Rock.
Mr. Microphone.
The Chia Pet.
OxiClean.
Pillow Pets.
The Snuggie!

You've seen these products on TV, probably with a smile on your face or a groan as you reach to change the channel. And although some of these "As Seen on TV" products can be quite amusing, their inventors are laughing, too… all the way to the bank.

The Pet Rock may have seemed like a "Why didn't I think of that?" idea, but in fact its inventor, Gary Dahl, was an advertising executive who saw an opportunity—a well-crafted, calculated opportunity—and took it….

And, while the "pet rock fad" lasted less than a year, the project was enough to make Dahl a millionaire many times over.

Who could ever forget the legendary tag line for the equally famous Mr. Microphone: "Hey, good lookin', I'll be back to pick you up later!" The phrase turns out to be just one of many originated by the legendary Ron Popeil, who many would credit as being the "father" of "As Seen on TV" advertising.

"Ch-ch-ch-chia!" The original Chia pet was a ram, which started the early 80s craze that continues to this day, producing such popular "Chias" as Homer Simpson and Shrek. The simple clay and seeds product, one of the first to gain national fame by being sold on TV, has made its producer Joseph Enterprises a nationally-recognized brand.

"Powered by the air you breathe, activated by the water that you and I drink," perhaps the pervasive Billy Mays' most infamous line, started a trend that would lead to billions of dollars in sales for OxiClean. What started on TV, soon led to Wal-Mart, Target and virtually every other retailer on the planet. Eventually, the company that launched OxiClean was sold by the Appel family for $325 million. You'll hear more of the OxiClean story in Chapter 1.

"It's a pillow. It's a pet. It's a Pillow Pet!" If you have children between the ages of 2 and 10, it's likely that you've heard them singing this tagline a few times around the house. You probably even have a Pillow Pet or two in your home. Jennifer Telfer, the inventor of the now famous Pillow Pet started selling the stuffed animal in malls in 2008 and quickly grew to $3 million in annual revenue. Not a bad start for a first time inventor. Two years later, in 2010, the Pillow Pets brand earned over $300 million in annual revenue, and it's still growing. This is a great example of how an inventor with a simple idea can turn their product into immense profits through selling on TV.

And, finally, who would believe that a blanket with sleeves would ever become a national phenomenon? But that's exactly what happened when the Snuggie was first introduced as a direct response commercial (infomercial) premiering in 2008. From there, the often-mocked—but wildly successful—product has been featured on the Today show and has grown to near cult-like status among its faithful followers.

What do these wildly differing products all have in common? For one, they were all initially sold on TV; and each has made its individual creators or companies millions. Chances are if you're reading a book called *Sell On TV*, you're at least vaguely familiar with pet rocks and Chia Pets, Mister Microphones, OxiClean, Pillow Pets and Snuggies, to say nothing of the Clapper, the Magic Jack, Ginsu knives and the PedEgg line of in-your-face commercials.

The fact is, love them or hate them, direct response TV commercials are a golden opportunity for inventors, salespeople and entrepreneurs… if you take a concerted, calculated and careful approach to the "business" of selling on TV.

My name is Jon LaClare, and I have made a business out of selling on TV. Today, I realize my dreams through helping inventors, entrepreneurs and growth-minded companies drive their products into what I call "hyper-growth." I do it through a company called Harvest Growth (www.HarvestGrowth.com) that I own with my energetic British business partner Jason Williams. Together, we've launched and managed products that now total over $1Billion in sales. Through the experience of successfully taking dozens of products to market, we've discovered several secrets that will help any consumer product be more successful. We're now ready to share these secrets to product launch success with you.

You see, launching a consumer product can help you earn millions of dollars very quickly, but it can also be a difficult task, especially if this is your first time treading these waters. Some entrepreneurs and inventors approach Harvest Growth wondering if they should pay someone to launch their product or do it themselves. There are essentially three basic go-to-market options once you determine that your product is right for selling on TV: "go it alone," hire a trusted advisor or license your product to a third party.

"Going it alone" includes market research, inventing, designing (product and packaging), prototyping, patenting, sourcing, costing, pricing, building a financial model (a realistic version!), developing a website, producing a Direct Response TV advertisement (a DRTV spot or "infomercial"), developing the back-end business including telemarketing, fulfillment and payment processing, buying media, tracking performance, pitching to retailers (I could write another book on that alone!) and running the day-to-day business. Many entrepreneurs are proficient at the early stages of product development, but they require help taking their products to market.

For many, it makes sense to work with someone with years of experience to hold your hands through the product launch process. Hiring outside expertise to guide you on your path to success helps you to avoid the common pitfalls, costly errors and wasted time that you're sure to encounter, and the cost is often less than you would think.

Why repeat the costly mistakes of others if you don't have to?

Another option is to license your product to a proven marketer that takes over all of the product development, day-to-day operations and financial risk and pays you a royalty based on the success of your product. We have found that the easiest and most profitable way to license your product is to perform a small test market to prove market demand. Once you have in-market results, licensees will compete against each other for your business.

In summary, it's your choice how involved you want to be in your product launch, but unless you are an experienced "marketeer," (marketing professional) you'll ultimately save time and earn more money if you work with someone with deep-rooted experience in launching products.

That's where ***Sell On TV: How to Sell Millions of Your Product On TV and in Retail*** comes in. Sell On TV shares years of knowledge as well as the secrets behind such brands as OxiClean to help you reap the benefits of winning sales models—and recreate their success stories—*without* reinventing the wheel.

Here is just some of what we'll be covering in *Sell on TV*:

- **A step-by-step guide to turning products into profits**
- **Laws of the Harvest (A proven methodology to predict the success of your product)**
- **Producing infomercials that sell**
- **TV to retail, the real road to riches**
- **Free advertising! How even billion-dollar brands are starting to use infomercial marketing**
- **How to increase your odds of success through market research**
- **Patents, trademarks and other legal mumbo jumbo**
- **Example financial projections for a successful launch**
- **And so much more...**

I wrote this book to help guide entrepreneurs and inventors in their quest to take their products to the masses. Having launched dozens of products for big companies and first-time inventors, I've seen the many pitfalls that can derail a product's launch.

The purpose of this book is to help you avoid those pitfalls and give your product the greatest chance for huge success. So if you're ready, a world of opportunity awaits.

Chapter 1

The OxiClean Story—From a Humble Garage to a $325million Payday

If you want to know the *true* power of selling your product successfully on TV, look no further than the $325,000,000 OxiClean success story. Although the OxiClean brand didn't fully penetrate the public consciousness until recently, the company's unmitigated success actually began decades ago— in a humble garage!

Humble Beginnings Don't Define—or Limit—Future Success

Orange Glo International (under its original name, Appel Mountain, Inc.) was founded by Max Appel in the 1980s. Max was more than just a businessman; he was an early environmentalist. Max had purchased a cleaning product from another company that he wanted to redesign and sell, but with one added ingredient: orange oil.

Max was concerned about the environmental impact of current cleaning agents, and wanted to create something less toxic and more beneficial for the environment. He had pledged to unleash the power of natural, toxic-free orange oil and though not a chemist by trade, began experimenting with various formulas in his family's garage.

The result was Orange Glo Wood Cleaner and Polish, the brainchild of Max's search for a toxin-free cleaning product. Each bottle contained the oily essence of 78 Valencia oranges and provided a fresh, appealing citrus smell that only enhanced the "green" nature of Max's brainchild.

From Creation to Sales: The Birth of a Brand

Having successfully created the product that would launch Orange Glo International, now all Max had to do was sell it. Fortunately, the closet chemist was also a professional salesman. Max had prior experience fundraising for various environmental organizations and medical centers, and now put his love of networking and creating long-term sales relationships to work selling his own product.

Max's wife, Elaine, came from a tax accounting and inventory management background and helped Max keep the books— as well as label, pack and ship the products! The husband and wife team struggled, for a time, to make the future Orange Glo International a success.

For the first few years, Max mixed the chemicals in his garage and, with Elaine's help, sold directly to consumers on the popular home show and county fair circuit. In fact, Orange Glo Wood Cleaner and Polish was demonstrated publicly for the first time in 1986 at the Arizona State Fair.

From there, consumer feedback urged Max to produce several variations of the orange oil based products, from cleaners for hard surfaces such as kitchen counters and stainless steel to industrial strength cleansers for pots and pans. With Max and Elaine working tirelessly from their Littleton, Colorado garage, revenues were still under $1million until 1997.

The Appels were sure they had a hit on their hands, but both kept their "day" jobs and worked full time until they felt they had enough regular and repeat business to work on their Orange Glo "empire" full-time.

Max sold OxiClean Stain Remover and Orange Glo wood polish at consumer home shows around the country for several years. The packed venues created a loud and raucous atmosphere that fit the born salesman's personality to a "T." Max wasn't alone in pitching his products for one and all to hear.

When Opportunity Meets Fate: A Powerful Partnership

In fact, he pitched several times right next to an energetic young pitchman named Billy Mays. Mays was a former walk-on linebacker for West Virginia University's football team.

Billy had started his sales career on the famed Atlantic City Boardwalk, hawking a product known as the Washmatik portable washing device to onlookers and passersby. The Washmatik was pitched as a hose that could actually pump water out of a bucket even though it wasn't attached to any faucet. Eventually, Billy took his act on the road and began selling a variety of maintenance products and tools on the same state fair and home show circuit as Max Appel.

The two converged once again on the day history was made. It happened at the 1993 Pittsburgh Home and Garden Show. Max and Billy were in adjacent booths, both pitching their products. Max was there with his Orange Glo cleaning products and Mays was once again pitching the Washmatik; his car washing system that didn't require a faucet. Billy had drawn a large crowd and was literally drowning out Max's sales pitch, which was suffering thanks to a broken microphone. To ease up on the competition, Billy loaned Max his spare microphone and actually turned down the volume on his. The two were good friends from that day forward. The friendship would turn out to benefit both in ways neither man could imagine.

The Family That Works Together, Earns Together

Max and Elaine's son Joel, who joined the business in 1991, and later his brother, David, both successfully helped the company, eventually known as Orange Glo Internationa, gain distribution in thousands of retail stores across the United States. By then, Max had patented his new product, OxiClean, and was finding gradual success with its revolutionary "oxygenated" cleaning formula.

However, despite being in approximately 10 percent of all retail outlets nationwide, and having a huge track record from years on the state fair and home show circuit, the OxiClean products failed to connect with the general public at first, mainly due to lack of major advertising.

The retail outlets helped, but only so much. The Appels found that they could get the product into the stores, but then the OxiClean would sit on the shelves. Nobody knew what to make of this brand new cleaning agent that had yet to discover its true "brand." In order to get the products off the shelves and into consumer's homes, the Appels decided they needed to get the word out.

Rather than spend millions on a traditional advertising budget through the regular media channels of print and television advertising,

Max and his family decided to take advantage of another revolutionary marketing channel: HSN, or the Home Shopping Network.

Pioneers and Pitchmen: The Birth of HSN

HSN had started as the "Home Shopping Club" in the early 80s, seen on local cable channels in Pinellas County, Florida. It became the first national shopping network in 1985, revolutionizing the way shoppers could view, phone and buy products right from the comfort of their own home.

In 1997, OxiClean first tested on the Home Shopping Network. It was OxiClean's first real experience with national advertising of any kind, let alone on live TV! When they needed a reliable, confident and effective TV pitchman, they first thought of Billy Mays.

The partnership between Billy's brash, positive and confident sales pitch with the OxiClean product was an instant success, selling 3,500 units the first day alone! It was a "perfect storm" of product (OxiClean) meeting pitchman (Billy Mays) meeting venue (HSN), and soon all three were household names.

Orange Glo International quickly ramped up to over 20,000 units per month of OxiClean and Orange Glo, and then soon added several other products like Power Paste, each also selling around 20,000 units per month. Revenues of Orange Glo products grew to $500,000 per month on HSN alone, and the business was now very profitable.

Direct Response Directly Responsible for Massive Profits

After their early and sustained success on HSN, Max and the rest of the Orange Glo International team decided to test a thirty minute "infomercial" in early 1998. The return was around a 2.0 MER (Media Efficiency Ratio), meaning that for every dollar the Appels spent on advertising, $2 were earned in revenue. They grew to spending $300,000 per month on TV, and reached total company revenues of over $300 million in 2002.

In 2000, after a competitor began selling a competitive product via 2 minute short form direct-response advertising, OxiClean produced its first 2-minute spot with Billy Mays. The MER declined slightly to range between 1.7 and 1.9, but the business was still profitable on TV, and awareness took off in a big way.

To put this achievement in proper perspective, remember: this was in an era where *100 percent of the revenues were received over the phones*! Forget banner ads and eBay and mouse clicks and Amazon.com. Website sales really didn't exist for this industry until the mid-2000s. Meanwhile, web sales now account for 50 percent or more of most campaigns (vs. telephone sales).

The short form (2 minute infomercial/spot) and long form (30 minute infomercials) advertising was a solid hit in the industry for Orange Glo International, and both forms of advertising ranked in the top 5 or 10 in the industry rankings Jordan Whitney and IMS (Infomercial Monitoring Service). Both are third party organizations that track media across dozens of networks to judge which products are spending the most on media (and are presumed to be the most successful). Retailers often use these ranking reports to decide which products to list in their stores (especially for the coveted "As Seen On TV" section of the stores so popular today).

The Retail Connection

With bigger numbers came bigger retailers. In late 1999, Sam's Club began selling OxiClean and, shortly thereafter, in early 2000, Wal-Mart picked up both OxiClean and Orange Glo. Suddenly, Max Appel had gone from blending orange oil in his garage to blanketing not just the airwaves but the shelves of the world's biggest retailers as well.

With TV advertising now in full swing, tubs of OxiClean and bottles of Orange Glo started to fly off the shelves, and other retailers began to take notice. Eventually, major retailers started to list many other products made by Orange Glo International. Today, of course, OxiClean and its many subsidiary products are sold in tens of thousands of retailers all over the country.

Much as the products made by Orange Glo International evolved over time, so did its success. Finding the right pitchman—Billy Mays—helped bring rapid success; finding the right medium, TV, helped bring national, then worldwide, name recognition. Meanwhile, the medium of TV advertising evolved as well.

Over time, advertising went from 30 minutes, to 2 minutes to 30 and 15 second advertisements. The short form, 30 second and 15 second advertising, was used to drive revenue growth in retail. Eventually the business was sold to Church & Dwight in July 2006 for

$325 million. All OxiClean TV advertising still featured Billy Mays until his untimely passing in the summer of 2010.

Parting Words about the OxiClean Success Story

The story of two very different men—Max Appel and Billy Mays— and their very similar rise to success via HSN and direct response TV marketing has within it the germ of everything you need to succeed by Selling on TV. What's missing is a repeatable system that can help you translate OxiClean's success into your own personal template for success.

Well, your own personal success system isn't missing any longer. The next chapter, in fact, provides a step-by-step guide for turning *products* into profits via direct response television marketing (DRTV)…

Chapter 2

How to Make Millions— 7 Steps to Turning Products into Profits

Many of today's most popular brand names, from Ginsu to OxiClean, had to find their secret to success through lots of costly trial and error. You can avoid the heartache, the time and the staggering cost by simply learning from their successes—and their failures.

Having helped brands like OxiClean and Nabisco craft their message and dominate market share, I've learned what it takes to create an effective, successful and above all repeatable system for making millions by turning your product(s) into profits. The good news is that you can do most of it cost-free, simply by harnessing good, old-fashioned muscle power and elbow grease and doing most of the legwork yourself.

No longer do you have to watch those late-night infomercials and think to yourself, "That should have been me!" Now it can be you, simply by following a handful of steps and fine-tuning your message before delivering it to the public.

Just like OxiClean, you can inexpensively bring your product to market and drive hyper growth through the power of direct response television marketing (DRTV).

Below I share for the very first time my *seven simple steps* to launching and growing revenues from your consumer product into the millions:

Step # 1: Market Research

The first step to creating a successful product is ensuring that the market actually *needs* that product in the first place. There's nothing worse than spending years creating something that, frankly, people just don't want—or need.

People come to us all the time with products they've invented or ideas they have, and a lot of times these inventions solve a real problem that the inventor has, but it doesn't impact many others.

Remember, your product doesn't have to necessarily be revolutionary or unique to stand out. There are probably hundreds of cleaning agents on the market today, but that didn't stop first OrangeGlo and then OxiClean from becoming big hits. Why? Because they had enough uniqueness to stand out in an otherwise crowded market.

So don't look at your grocery store or department store shelves and think, "Ah, this product already exists." Look at your product and see how it can be better, more unique, more marketable than anything else out there. Of course, it helps to have something brand new—but only if it's something consumers are going to actually want—and buy!

In order for your product to become a big hit on DRTV, you need to make sure it works for a mass market. OxiClean, for example, can be used by every home in America, and in most of the rest of the world. As a contrast, a baby product targeted to children aged 1 to 2 is a very limited market, and it is very difficult to profitably market to such a small audience via television advertising. That sounds intimidating at first, but the fact of the matter is that as large as the "mass market" is, it's actually populated by individuals. One person ordering Magic Jack here, another ordering a musical snow globe off HSN there. So chances are if you can find a lot of separate individuals who are interested in your product, the mass market will be interested as well.

So, where do you start? Right in your own backyard, that's where. First, talk to people you know, such as your friends and family. Let them know the basics of your product, invention or idea; what it does, who it's for, why it's different. It's best to write a "concept," or a description of the product, outlining the key features and benefits of the product to share with people. You might even print them on a business card to quickly share with people and ask for feedback.

Next, talk to people at work, to neighbors, to people in your church groups, book clubs or gym. Firsthand research like this is nearly as effective as professional focus groups, which can cost thousands of dollars—and it yields very similar results.

What is the value in this exercise? What you're looking for is to answer a series of six basic questions that will help you not only refine your existing product but also make it more suitable for the mass market. This turns a simple Q & A over the back fence or by the water cooler into what is known a "market research." And, as anyone in the field can tell you, such research is worth its weight in gold!

Be formulaic in your questions so you ask the same basic questions to everyone. This way you're getting targeted feedback on the following six very specific questions:

- "When and where would you use this?"
- "What problem does it solve?"
- "Have you seen anything else on the market similar to this?"
- "Would you buy this, and how much would you be willing to pay?"
- "What do you like best about this product?"
- "What can be improved?"

Step # 2: Identify the key features and benefits

- **"What makes you stand out from the crowd?"**
- **"What makes you different from a dozen other cleaning products, running shoes, sports drinks or inflatable stadium seats on the market today?"**
- **"What distinguishes you as a brand?"**

These are just a few of the questions you'll need to ask in Step 2. We'll start with identifying two major factors that will help to bring character and brand recognition to your product/invention:

1.) **Features**: Features are the specific qualities that pertain to a particular product. They are the facts that aren't open to interpretation. For instance, what does the product do, how does it work, what is it made of, what color is it, etc. If you were to list the features of, say, a popular protein bar they would be things like peanut butter, chocolate, 23 grams of protein, 14 grams of carbs, 9 grams of sugar, all-natural, etc.

So features are what physically describe your product in a very real and literal sense.

2.) **Benefits**: Benefits are what the product actually "does" for the consumer, although they are directly linked back to the features (above). To determine what a particular benefit might be, ask "why does that matter" for each of the features. For instance, why do "23 grams of protein" matter for the consumer? High protein diets can help you lose weight. "Why does that matter? When you maintain a healthier weight, you feel better. So, what might be a key benefit statement for this protein bar: "look and feel better when you eat _____." You can always turn a feature into a benefit by simply asking, "why does that matter?" Too often, inventors spend too much time talking about the features of their products, so consumers turn a blind eye. If they changed their focus to true benefits, the target audience would then become truly engaged. Every time you mention a feature ask yourself "why does that matter?"

Features and their *benefits* are like talking points for your product; they give you things to talk about in press releases, at trade shows, to potential investors and when marketing and promoting your product. Here is a great example of a nationally-known product and why its features and benefits matter:

New Planters Almonds are slow roasted and sprinkled with 100 percent pure sea salt.

Now, let's analyze two of its main features—"slow-roasted" and "100 percent pure sea salt"—to see what benefits those might provide to hungry consumers:

1.) **Slow roasting:** *Why does that matter?* The slow roasting process delivers flavor throughout the entire nut.
    o Why does *that* matter? The nut tastes more delicious and fresher than other almonds.

2.) **Sea salt:** *Why does that matter?* Sea salt is better for your body than table salt, and it delivers a stronger flavor than table salt.

- o Why does *that* matter? You can use less salt and still have a strong flavor.
- o Why does *that* matter? Our new almonds taste better and are better for you.

Once you clearly identify a product's five to ten "features," you can no doubt provide an endless array of "benefits" that keep branching out into more and more benefits for the average consumer.

So you see, mining your product or invention for as many features and benefits as possible is going to provide you with a veritable "laundry list" of talking points when it comes time to promote your product successfully via DRTV.

Step # 3: Test Market

Until you actually get the product in the hands of actual consumers, all of the above is just theory. After all, you can have dozens of healthy, all-natural, organic, "green" features and benefits but if your revolutionary new protein bar tastes like sawdust, well, consumers won't care if it has the lowest sugar content on the market—OR the most protein.

To give your product a "live dress rehearsal" so to speak, you will want to test market the product at events where your target market—real, live people who are likely to be interested in purchasing it—can actually touch, feel and taste what you have to offer.

You think OxiClean came to market in the exact shape and form that it eventually took? Hardly; it was test marketed repeatedly to smooth out the bumps in the road, fine tune the mixture, improve the smell, the packaging—and whatever else didn't quite "work."

OxiClean was sold in home shows to learn what consumers liked and didn't like about the product so it could be constantly improved; not just the scientific formula or "recipe," but also the marketing language.

By testing out various ads, slogans, posters and language, the makers of OxiClean were able to quickly and successfully pick and choose which features and benefits mattered most—to the customers who mattered most.

Where can you most effectively test market your product or invention? Here is a list of viable venues to start:

- **Home shows**
- **Trade shows**
- **State fairs**
- **Flea markets**
- **A website**
- **Niche catalogs**
- **Specialty retailers**
- **Local mom and pop stores**
- **Etc.**

Step # 4: Develop the Key Messaging for Your Advertising Campaign from the Knowledge You Have Gained So Far

Now that you're halfway through my 7-step process, it's time to develop what I call the "key messaging" for your advertising campaign. Use what you've already learned from the three previous steps—market research, key features and benefits, test market—to refine the message so that it sounds professional, appealing and ultimately marketable.

To see a template for success, look at how other products in your niche market themselves. Memorize the web copy or product packaging for your favorite products and use them to guide your own.

Learn what works for you by continuing to field test various slogans or signage. For instance, as you travel to flea markets or home shows or specialty retailers in the region, see what's working for others and note it while you also determine what works best for you. Maybe you don't need three posters around your booth; maybe only one will do. That will save you costs down the road, and help you to make the one poster count.

Maybe that long-winded slogan you cooked up late one night is too long; maybe by continuing to edit it down you can settle on a quick, simple, 5-word slogan that is so catchy people start remembering it even when they don't see it.

Do the kind of advertising that works for you. Some products are indistinguishable from their inventors—or their pitchmen. If you're more comfortable inventing products than pitching them, help the product speak for itself with marketing that draws on its own unique features and benefits versus your own.

Step # 5: Produce an Infomercial and Test on National Cable Television

Of course, the home show, flea market and state fair circuit is a great way to field test and dress rehearse your product, but you bought this book because you want to "Sell on TV," and that's where Step 5 comes in!

I know it can sound daunting, but if you've come this far, then the time is now to go the rest of the way. And the fact is, you don't need to do it all on your own. In fact, I wouldn't even recommend it!

That's right, I'll tell you what I tell all our clients: *Don't attempt this step without the help of a professional.* There are several top-tier infomercial producers that minimize your costs when they believe in your product.

These are qualified, credible industry experts who will give you the same kind of quality and expertise as you see on other DRTV products—at a fraction of the cost. This way, it doesn't have to cost you an arm and leg upfront to produce an exceptional DRTV creative.

In fact, producers in the DRTV industry earn most of their money from royalties paid from product revenues. This helps to minimize your upfront costs and helps to make sure the producer has "skin in the game," so to speak. Earning royalties on the back end helps ensure that your DRTV producer will produce a quality creative as that will help both of you make money.

Many inventors have tried to produce their own infomercial. And why not? After all, the rise of modern technology and the affordability of lights, soundstages and even camcorders have made this mission-critical step appear "easy."

Unfortunately, just as many have failed. Producing a quality, marketable DRTV spot requires more than an empty soundstage and good lighting; it requires a targeted script, skilled pitchman, breakneck timing, a competent editor and about 1,001 other aspects that could fill another book! As an example, we once worked with a client that had a fantastic product, but they had previously failed on TV. We completely re-scripted their spot, and when it went back on air, the results increased by over 500 percent! Working with someone that knows what they're doing in the DRTV industry can make the difference between a success and a failure.

Advertising media can be just as important as the production. That's why there is great value in hiring an expert to handle this critical task as well. If you're unsure where to start, don't just hire any media agency; hire a media agency that specializes in *direct-response TV media*. Just like social media differs from traditional print or radio media, direct-response media is very different from normal television advertising media.

The agency you select needs to understand this market, so hire carefully. They need to know what stations work for each product category. Several media agencies exist that successfully book over $100MM in DRTV media annually for various clients.

Once you have a professionally-produced video spot, next "test" it in appropriate markets where your product will hopefully find a home. A typical media test will cost $10,000, your spot will air 50 to 100 times across 6 to 10 national cable TV stations and you will obtain a very clear picture of your return-on-investment. When you are successful with a test, the media is scalable. In other words, you can increase your spend and remain confident that your returns will continue to be profitable. Be sure to test different times of day using different TV station genres. A reputable DRTV media agency will manage all of this for you. When done right and tracked carefully, this media buy will result in massive exposure for your product and reap huge potential profits.

Step # 6: Produce Profitable Results

Step 6 finds us crunching numbers to determine the profitability of your test runs to date. When your media test is profitable, you can generally expect around a 2x return on your media spend; equaling twice what you put in.

So, for instance, if you spend $10,000, you could earn $20,000—or 2x the buy-in. If you are in that range, congratulations! Obviously, you have a winner on your hands and all your hard work has paid off.

When this is the case, it becomes much easier to pitch to major retailers like Target, Wal-Mart, Walgreens, Bed Bath & Beyond and others. This is where you see entire displays devoted to the recognizable "As Seen on TV" logo. This is priceless shelf-space for any DRTV product.

I know what you're thinking: "Hey, isn't this book called *Sell On TV?*" Absolutely, but a result of the successful merge from television to retail is a tidal wave of profits not earned directly via DRTV. Case in point: for every $1 earned on TV, you will typically earn $5 to $10 in retail. Also, your profit margins will increase as you move into wide retail distribution.

So when it comes to TV, remember that while there is (much) profit to be made, the real pot of gold typically exists in retail. Set your sights accordingly, and view TV as your enter into this lucrative retail environment.

Ramp up your spending either organically (i.e. reinvesting the profits each week), or by getting financing from your media results, which is very common in the DRTV industry.

Remember, you're not really "spending" money on a successful DRTV campaign; you're investing it. With a 2x buy-in ratio, you're making money every time you "spend" it, which is critical to your ultimate success.

After all, the more you are able to spend, the more immediate DRTV revenue you will see come in—and the faster you'll be able to get into retail. Ultimately, this will deliver you a very strong overall cash flow.

Step # 7: Repeat the process all over again

The real secret to DRTV success—and ultimately being able to *Sell on TV*—is in finding a repeatable process—and then working it over and over again. Key to repetition is keeping what works, and throwing out what doesn't.

OxiClean was successful, in part, because they constantly searched for product improvements and new products to launch. They knew they had a system that worked, and a brand name to build on.

Once trust in first the OrangeGlo brand and, later, the OxiClean brand was established, they could continually refine and test new products using the system they'd established for both successful products.

It's a little like perfecting a great icing recipe. It may take weeks, even months, of trial and error to come up with the perfect blend of richness, texture, creaminess, thickness and sweetness, but once you do—the cake icing world is yours for the taking. You now have a repeatable system and you can turn that icing any color you want—and trust that it will bear the properties that made your first batch successful.

In fact, that's just what Gwen Willhite, the founder and CEO of Cookies by Design did. Eager to combine two popular gifts, cookies and flowers, into one proved harder than she first imagined. Sending cookies by mail, key to the Cookies by Design franchise model, required a very specific kind of cookie; tough enough to stand up to shipping all over the country but moist, sweet and soft enough to be enjoyed by its recipients! The frosting also had to be the perfect blend of tasty and functional.

Gwen tried dozens of recipes before she struck on the eventual winning secret, but once she did—all that hard work paid off by being able to be repeated time and time again, not just in her own kitchen—where her company started—but in hundreds of franchise locations across the country.

Franchises are the ultimate repeatable systems. We want to be able to walk into a Burger King in Florida or Fresno and get the same exact Whopper—every time. And why should the stock in a Miami Old Navy be different from that of one in, say, Beverly Hills? Building on the same simple cookie and icing recipe, Gwen Willhite was able to successfully brand—and franchise—her popular Cookies by design company. And the rest is history!

In your case, it's not icing your perfecting but a series of simple steps that you can now repeat, over and over again, to similar success. The product may change, but the system you use to market it, promote it, sell it on TV and, ultimately, into the retail market will remain essentially the same because it's repeatable. Now, once you understand the system, you can grow your business by launching more products.

Chapter 3

The 7 Laws of the Harvest

You can't just plant a seed in the ground, walk away, come back six months later and expect it to become the next giant beanstalk! To look forward to a plentiful harvest, you must follow several "laws" to ensure that your seed grows into strong, healthy profit.

The seed must be tended, tilled, watered and encouraged. Weather conditions must follow a consistent pattern and, if they don't, you must *take matters into your own hands* to ensure that Mother Nature doesn't interfere with your harvest.

Much as a seed grows into an ear of corn, then rows of corn, and finally corn stalks that must be harvested, brought to market and sold before they can become wheat—and profit—for the farmer, so too does the modern inventor, creator, salesperson or entrepreneur need to follow several "rules of the harvest" to ensure that their idea grows into a bountiful profit source as well; 7 laws to be exact:

The 7 Laws of the Harvest

The 7 Laws of the Harvest are a proven methodology to predict the success of your product. While chance plays a part in every success story—what if Max Appel hadn't ever met Billy Mays, for instance?—there are rules, "laws" if you will, that we can follow to ensure success against formidable odds.

When we at Harvest Growth analyze new products to see if they will be a success in the DRTV industry, we look to the following key criteria to help us determine their potential for success. As a general rule, you should be able to answer a resounding "Yes" to most, if not all, of the seven following questions:

The First Law: Is Your Product UNIQUE?

First and foremost, the product must be *different* and *new*. That means it must be something most people haven't seen before, or something most people "think" they haven't seen before. There have been many successful products that were not first to market, but the consumers simply weren't aware of the preceding product.

For instance, the Snuggie ® first existed as the Slanket ®, which successfully generated revenues in the hundreds of thousands. The Snuggie ®, however, when launched via DRTV, generated revenue in excess of $100 million in its first year.

How? By rebranding itself to seem "brand" new. You see the "uniqueness" factor in movies, music and TV all the time. James Bond is far from "new" or "unique," for instance, but in stripping away the cheesy one-liners and soap opera clichés, the "new and improved" Daniel Craig managed to breathe new life into a franchise that had grown stagnant and stale. The creative team behind the latest two Bond movies, Casino Royale and Quantum of Solace, were able to capture huge box office share by being seen as unique in the marketplace.

Meanwhile, pop stars Jessica Simpson and Jewel breathed new life into their careers by releasing country albums that were neither new or unique, but new and unique... for them.

As you can see, marketing will have a lot to do with helping people create strong perceptions about your product. If it actually "is" new and unique, such as the first-ever "inkless" pen or the revolutionary new waterproof underwear, then it will pretty much market itself.

But if you're looking at something in a new light and seeing a new use for it, then be sure to adopt a more aggressive and realistic marketing campaign to add newness and uniqueness to an existing product, much as the mildly-successful Slanket ® evolved into the wildly-popular Snuggie ®.

The Second Law: Does Your Product Fit a MASS MARKET?

To become a DRTV success story, your product *must* appeal to a large enough market. Local, niche or "specialty" products that only appeal to one demographic seldom succeed. This is the age old problem of an inventor developing the best product in the world to solve a problem that only he and his neighbor experience.

While your patented, scent-fee alligator repellent may sell well at local flea markets in South Florida, why would the average housewife in, say, Minnesota or Wisconsin, stay-tuned to your DRTV commercial?

Face it: *she wouldn't*. Nor would folks in the northeast or, for that matter, the southwest. Which isn't to say that you won't do gangbusters with your product locally, but which *is* to say that it may not be the best product for a DRTV ad.

To work on TV, you need to be able to sell to a very wide audience. Don't get me wrong; it doesn't have to appeal to everybody. While most men have heard of OxiClean, few have ever bought the product. But American women are a large enough viewing audience to ensure that the OxiClean brand would become successful even though its audience is more specific to women; it is also very wide because all kinds of women buy the product.

Even something like the Chia Pet, which is still going strong today, has mass appeal. Not only are offshoots like Chia Sponge Bob popular with children, but you can see Chia Scooby Doos in dorm rooms all over the country and Chia Homer Simpsons in office cubicles nationwide.

Again, appealing to a "wide" audience doesn't mean it has to appeal to everyone on the planet. But do your research to ensure that there is a big enough, a wide enough, audience to ensure DRTV success *before* you invest in a DRTV ad.

The Third Law: Does Your Product <u>SOLVE A PROBLEM</u>?

Your product has to solve a perceived problem that doesn't already have a good-enough solution. Aspirational, or luxury, products just don't play on DRTV. The kind of people who will buy something they see on TV by calling into a telemarketing center or visiting a website almost immediately after viewing the infomercial want the product to solve a problem, not necessarily make them "feel" better.

Ask yourself, would you rather have a $9.95 hose attachment that allows you to clean second story windows without having to climb out on your roof, or a $59.95 collection of the world's greatest literary works? Sure, it'd be "nice" to have leather bound volume of Dickens and Hemingway, but spring is coming and I "really" need to get those upstairs windows clean to enjoy the first blue skies of the new year.

That's how people—*real* people—think, and that's the kind of "need first, want second" philosophy that makes practical, problem-solving products so popular "as seen on TV."

This is why 90 percent of successful DRTV creative sessions start out with a problem/solution approach. Identify the problem and show how your product solves this problem.

The Ped Egg (portable and effective callous remover for your foot) is a perfect example of a product that solves an age-old problem, drying and cracked feet, that nearly everyone has. That's why it became one of the biggest product launch successes of all time.

The Fourth Law: Is Your Product **PRICED RIGHT**?

Think of the most popular items you see on TV, from the Slap Chop to the Sham Wow to the Ped Egg and beyond. Chances are you know how much they cost, if not down to the penny.

$10?

$14.99?

Or $19.99?

90 percent of successful short form (2-minute) TV spots have products priced at $19.99—or below. Occasionally, you'll see higher priced items, like exercise equipment, but they generally have to provide a cheaper "trial offer" or multiple payment plans to make the offer reasonable.

As with all of the criteria, there are always wildly successful exceptions to the rule. You also want to make sure your product is highly valued. When it is sold for $20, it needs to appear to be an amazing deal.

The Fifth Law: Can Your Product be **EASILY EXPLAINED**?

People need to be able to understand what your product does quickly. The best way to accomplish this feat is to select products that are simple and highly demonstrable.

Can you whip it out of your briefcase in an elevator and demonstrate it by the time you get to the fifth floor? Can you show a simple prototype, mock-up or drawing and get people nodding their heads in recognition? These are the signs of an easily-explained, demonstrable, relatable product that will succeed via DRTV.

In other words, always be thinking of your "elevator" pitch. An elevator pitch is a quick, 5- to 10-second phrase you can use to describe your product to any audience, at any time, at the drop of a hat.

A typical elevator pitch will sound something like:

- **A portable pedicure shaped like an egg that fits in your purse**
- **A weatherproof hose attachment that allows you to clean second-story windows**
- **A lovable "pet" that requires no food, water or even shelter**
- **A revolutionary new cleaning product that uses the power of oxygen to remove stains**

Visual demonstrations of how your product works can be even more powerful. If your product just sits there and doesn't do anything, it will be difficult to keep an audience interested in a two-minute television spot. Try to determine the best way to demonstrate how your product works by showing it to friends and family. If they are amazed, it's a good probability that America will be amazed as well.

Conversely, if your product takes too long to explain or demonstrate, even with a full 2-minute TV spot most viewers won't "get it" and will stop trying long before the commercial is over.

The Sixth Law: Is Your Product Targeted to the Right AGE DEMOGRAPHIC?

What age group would be most interested in your product? Before you answer, know this: it should appeal to people over the age of 50, or at least not exclude this group. That's because the typical DRTV buyer is in this demographic.

Now, before you throw your hands up in frustration, remember: many men and women over the age of 50 are more than just senior citizens. They are also:

- **Hobbyists**
- **Parents**
- **Grandparents**
- **Campers**
- **Gardeners**
- **Coin collectors**
- **Car washers**
- **Volunteers**
- **Etc.**

This means that even if a Pillow Pet or a Bumpits hair clip might not appeal to them directly, they can certainly be thinking of Christmas gifts for their children or birthday gifts for their grandchildren.

They might want one PedEgg for themselves—and another for their daughter-in-law. Maybe they're going to use that hose-slash-wand attachment to clean their own second story windows, or donate it to the church. Either way, by including this popular and ready-to-buy segment in planning for your DRTV ad, you will increase your odds of reaping a profit when you harvest!

The Seventh Law: Is Your Product <u>CREDIBLE</u>?

Finally, people must absolutely, 100 percent believe that your product will work "as advertised." Many DRTV items that meet the previous six criteria fail here because the promise they make just isn't believable.

While the popular misconception is that gullible late-night TV viewing audiences will gobble up any old product that meets a need and is under $20, the fact is audiences are savvier than ever.

Even if you "do" manage to dupe an audience into believing something looks better than it actually is, today's consumers will not only return shabby merchandise immediately but, thanks to the power of social media, will promptly tell their Facebook "friends" and Twitter "followers" about the experience—often to your detriment.

The "magic" of TV is such that items can look bigger, smaller, brighter, shinier, cooler, faster and all-around "better" than they do in real-life. However, one thing TV shouldn't do is make a flimsy, unstable or accident-prone product look effective on national TV.

Parting Words about the 7 Laws of the Harvest

Just like any harvest, you want to reap big rewards for your effort. Chances are you've thought long and hard, and planned and product-tested longer and harder, on your idea before beginning to read this book.

Knowing the 7 Laws of the Harvest now will help you reap bigger profits later by helping you trouble-shoot your product before you go to the added expense of shooting a DRTV ad.

Even if you haven't been able to answer all of the above questions with a resounding "yes," at least now you know where your failings are so that you can go in and rectify them before it hits the airwaves—or retail shelves.

Don't be discouraged; the products that meet these 7 criteria are much more likely to succeed than those who don't, and by taking the time to perfect them now you will increase your profit tenfold in the future.

Chapter 4

10 Steps for Producing Infomercials That Sell

Many late-night TV ads might look impressive, sophisticated and costly, but did you know that launching a direct-response marketing campaign can cost less than $50,000, all in? Imagine that for the price of a luxury sedan, a boat or that new home improvement project you were planning for next year, you can launch a DRTV ad that could revolutionize the way you live.

Of course it's still a significant investment, but if you carefully follow the 7 Laws of the Harvest I've just shared, as well as the rest of the valuable information you'll find in this book, I'm sure you'll agree the profit potential is well worth the investment.

Of course, there are varying lengths of DRTV ad creatives you might want to run, including long-form infomercials that run up to 30-minutes and shorter form DRTV spots that run for two-minutes.

Specifically, 2-minute DRTV spots are a great testing ground for product launches. They also help to drive national brand awareness more efficiently than any other marketing vehicle.

Of course, the more time you spend on air, the more it's going to cost you. How much more are we talking about here? Half-hour productions can cost anywhere between $100,000 and $1,000,000, just for the production!

Not in your budget at this time? No worries. You can produce a high quality two-minute spot with many of the best producers in the industry for as little $30,000 to $40,000. Then, when you're ready to go to market, each national cable television media test will cost approximately $10,000.

Post-production, meaning once the actual half-hour spot is filmed, cut and edited, there are additional considerations. These extra fees include what it will cost to actually process, package and ship (or fulfill) the orders that come in as a result of the ad (known as "fulfillment") plus the 1-800 operators you'll need to man the phones before, during and after the ad (telemarketing) and you'll also want web support and development for those who would rather order online (website development).

In total, an average of around $50,000 for a national launch of your product? It sounds too good to be true, especially considering Kraft, Proctor & Gamble and others can invest over $2 million or more in a single product launch (even if unsuccessful). You would think that the success rate for the "big guys" would be higher, but it's not. DR products have about a 10 percent to 15 percent chance of being a home run, whereas the big consumer product companies' average is a bit lower.

The fact is, while social media is the "new kid on the block" for product promotion, many marketers are missing the boat by ignoring DRTV as a valuable, affordable and profitable way to bridge the gap between TV and retail.

The real question is, "Why doesn't every consumer product marketer use direct-response as a launching pad for their products?" Good question! Before the rest of the world finds out about this incredible way to market your product to the world, take advantage of it now by following the **10 Steps to Producing Infomercials That Sell**:

Step 1: Start with a Problem-Solving Opening

What problem does your product solve?

A stained blouse, an easier way to scoop up pet waste or a portable pedicure?

How will it help the consumer in his or her everyday life?

Wash his car when no hose is available, provide a magnetic screwdriver tip that helps keep the screws in place in hard-to-reach areas or allow him or her to go fishing on his or her lunch break with your portable rod, reel and bait?

These are the questions you should be answering, not just for yourself but in the opening frames of your DRTV ad. That's Step # 1: Start with a problem-solution opening.

Most successful DRTV products solve a problem. Making that problem seem as painful as possible helps create the impulse to purchase and positions your product as the hero of the commercial.

The classic line for this part of the commercial: "Are you tired of...."

Here are some common questions you might begin your DRTV spot with:

- "Are you tired of... dirty windows that are too high to reach?"
- "Are you tired of... costly pedicures that take too long?"
- "Are you tired of... getting sore knees after only 10 minutes in your garden?"
- "Are you tired of... knives that are too dull to cut through a tomato?"
- "Are you tired of... jar lids that just won't open?"
- "Are you tired of... soda that goes too flat, too soon?"

Posing a problem and offering your product as the solution is a great one-two opening for any DRTV ad, and for just about any product!

Step 2: Showcase Unique Features and Benefits

We've already discussed the unique features and benefits of your product in the *7 Laws of the Harvest* section, but now it's important to make the features and benefits of your product appear to be as different as possible from other products on the market.

Now that you've presented a problem and your product as a solution (see Step # 1, above), you are starting to draw in the consumer and get them excited about your product. Keep them interested—and from turning the channel—by making them believe that your product has features and benefits that they can't live without!

Lists are helpful in this area. For instance, let's say your revolutionary new padded garden kneeler is great for older gardeners or those with sore knees who still want to get out in the garden. Well, that's great, but... no doubt there are several of those on the market already. So... how will you stand out?

Perhaps your garden kneeler comes with a sleeve for inserting heating pads during cold weather, or ice packs during spring and summer! Hey, great; list those! Maybe it's waterproof and easy to clean; list that! Maybe it comes with reversible covers so you can match your knee pad to your outfit; list that! Maybe you can personalize it; list that!

I'm sure now you can see how with just some creative thinking and out of the box brainstorming, you can provide additional features and benefits to make your one-of-a-kind product truly necessary in today's modern world.

Step 3: Demonstrate the Product Repeatedly and Feature a "Magic" Demo

Products sold on TV can lack credibility. It's hard for folks to reach out and touch a product marketed on TV, and so they are often understandably doubtful. Unlike a real, live demonstration at a mall, say, or flea market or home show, TV viewers often ask, "Yeah, it *looks* great, but... does it *really* work?"

Product demonstrations help the consumer to feel confident that your product will perform as promised. These "demos" are best performed in a setting that makes them appear "live" and without trickery. Changing camera angles or doing jump cuts in the editing room all bring doubt to the mind of the consumer. The slicker the polish, the fancier the edits, the more "produced" a segment looks, the less likely a consumer is to believe it's actually happening for real. They want to see the "magic" happen, the knife slice through the tomato, the beer can or the phone book, from start to finish!

"Magic demos" are the ones that are the most memorable, that get people's attention, that prove without a doubt your product works and that get them reaching for the phone to order your product—NOW, if not sooner!

Perhaps the most powerful demo of all time was the "fishbowl" demo with Billy Mays and OxiClean. To refresh your memory, Billy had a bowl filled with black water, poured a small scoop of OxiClean into the bowl, swished it around with his hands, and like magic, the water turned clear... instantly! It was simple, powerful and very, very effective.

In fact, many market analysts—myself included!—credit the billions of dollars that OxiClean eventually sold to this one magical, unforgettable demo. Likewise, if you develop a demo that is powerful and memorable like this... you'll have a winner on your hands!

Step 4: Explain How the Product Works

How does someone slip in a heating pack to your padded gardening kneepad?

How does someone slide on the nozzle for your magic window sprayer?

How does someone use your portable pedicure egg?

Explaining how the product works, in language that is simple and easy to follow, is the next step in producing infomercials that sell. If viewers are confused, they will never buy. How do other DRTV ads handle this dilemma? The most common language is:

- "It's as easy as 1... 2... 3..."
- "The secret is..."
- "Watch how we...."
- "Simply turn the cap and..."
- "With three quick snaps you're in business..."

Etc. In addition to the live demo we just discussed in Step 3, animation works really well to show how a product works. For instance, using arrows or numbers or even the word "click" you can easily show how the products works by highlighting each step.

Step 5: Prove the Efficacy of the Product with Comparisons

One way to prove just how effective your product is, is to compare it with other similar products. A typical method of comparing is the side-by-side demo, which pits your product against a competitor or older method.

So, maybe your heated gardening kneepad is twice as thick as anything else on the market. Prove it! How? By comparing it in thickness to several representative brands. You can show yours on the left, at five inches thick, and line the competitors up in varying degrees of thickness to show how, clearly, yours actually IS the thickest on the market!

Or let's say you are offering a "Miracle Grow" type product that produces vegetables two or three times the size of those grown without your product. Prove it by showing your tomatoes next to smaller tomatoes, your heads of lettuce next to other heads of lettuce, etc.

Another typical method of contrasting is before-and after photography (often shown in a split screen). So maybe your portable pedicure system is safe, affordable and effective. One way to prove that is to show a woman's foot before the pedicure, and after.

Step 6: Establish Credibility with Testimonials or Endorsements

If you've ever seen a former pro football player discussing the effectiveness of a certain arthritis cream, a former astronaut shilling golf balls or an older actor talking about denture cream, then you know just how effective consumer testimonials and celebrity endorsements can be to helping provide credibility and a little "star power" to a product.

Testimonials are powerful in bringing credibility to your product. When the person is similar to us, we trust them. This is a powerful emotion in consumers. It's why you see regular senior citizens talking about their experience with hearing aids, motorized wheelchairs or, in your case, a heated gardening pad!

It's why you see young, hip, active, outdoorsy types bragging about a great pair of wrap-around shades with revolutionary tinted lenses, etc. For endorsements, you can use celebrities to bring attention to your brand or third-party seals of approval.

Step 7: Raise and Answer Obvious Questions or Concerns

Consumers are skeptical. It's only human nature that they will be asking if your product is legitimate. Even if they've seen a live demonstration of your knife cutting through beer cans or a 12-pound tomato, to get all this for $19.99 or less would make anyone suspicious.

If you raise the common questions or concerns in the infomercial, you can ease their concerns before they become too dire—or before they change the channel. Just be careful not to raise a question that they wouldn't have thought of or, worse yet, a concern that you cannot effectively address.

For instance, a common concern raised by revolutionary new products is, "It sounds too good to be true..." If your product raises this issue, address it! Have your announcer say, "Think it's good to be true? It's not, and here's why..." And then tell them why.

Here are some other obvious examples of the types of questions or concerns you might want to consider raising—and answering/addressing—before your consumer audience has the chance to do it for you:

- "Here's proof that our super bond glue is twice as strong as the rest..."
- "Here's how safe our double-jointed ladder can be..."
- "Look how our patented single-edge blade won't break the skin..."
- Etc.

Step 8: Craft a High Value Offer

DRTV buyers are very price sensitive... they are always looking for a great deal and if you spend an evening watching DRTV spots, you'll see that the price point is very uniform. Great deals include such incentives as premiums, or bonus items. If you can include such premiums in your offer, they are a great way of increasing value.

Here are some other ways to craft a high power offer that, if built carefully—and attractively—enough, will prove irresistible to consumers:

- **Double the offer:** Double offers are very powerful. So, instead of selling one waterproof flashlight that also doubles as a camping lantern and space heater for $9.99, offer two flashlights for $14.99.
- **Pile it on:** We have all seen campaigns double their returns by changing a price point or the structure of their offer. This can be the most important aspect of the creative sell-through. For instance, viewers might not be induced to buy a waterproof flashlight on its own, but when you get creative you can provide more add-ons to increase the value. "But wait, there's more..." or "But we're not done yet!..." are some of our favorite lines to show this high value. So you show them the flashlight, show them one more—

because they're getting 2-for-1—then add, one at a time, a matching raincoat, a waterproof hat, not one but two rechargeable batteries... you get the picture.

- **Compare creatively:** Finally, you can help to increase the perceived value of your product by comparing to competitive products: "A similar product could cost as much as $50, but you can buy ours for only $19.99!"

Step 9: Minimize the Risk with a Money Back Guarantee

Have you ever wondered why most DRTV ads feature a "money back" guarantee at the end? Here's why: you help minimize the consumer's risk, or at least their perceived risk, by making it a "risk free" offer. Get your money back? Who wouldn't buy your product if it's a risk free purchase?

At a minimum, there should be a money-back guarantee offered to increase the purchase conversion of your DRTV product. However, money-back guarantees are so commonplace these days that they don't add a lot of value by themselves.

What's more, many companies charge for postage when returning a product, taking some of that "money back" away from the frustrated consumer, which naturally only makes them "more" frustrated!

Give your guarantee more "teeth" by making it painless, easy and proven with the classic line: "If you aren't completely satisfied, send it back for a full refund of the purchase price." Consider paying for the return postage if you feel there will be credibility hurdles for you to get over. Play around with different guarantee language if you feel it will be an important purchase driver for your particular product. The guarantee is generally a given, but if creatively worded, it can add tremendous value to your campaign.

Step 10: Don't Forget the Backend!

Once the commercial is created (otherwise called "the creative") your work is just beginning. Why's that? Well, even if you produce the perfect creative, you can still fall flat on your face if you don't have the right website, telemarketing script or media plan in support of the DRTV ad you spent so much time, money and effort on. It is crucial that you choose the right vendors for each of these areas. They literally can make or break your campaign.

Parting Words about Producing Infomercials That Sell

Clearly, infomercials and other DRTV ads are a great way to get your product seen by millions of potential customers. Ask any company, inventor or marketing expert and they'll tell you that to reach millions of consumers for $50,000 or less—all in—is a great bargain in anybody's price range.

It's always amazing to me when clients will drive up in $100,000 cars they didn't think twice of buying, then balk at producing a TV spot that costs half as much—and has the potential to take their business to the next level and beyond.

Clearly, much goes into producing a TV spot; any TV spot. Regardless of length, there is set design, casting, scripting, recording, lighting, electricians, editing, sound... the list goes on. Like any good marketing decisions, seek experts who know their craft.

Find a quality production company who can help you through this challenging but worthwhile process. Check their references, like you would any other company you were going to spend $50,000 with, and be sure to see their portfolio of the DRTV commercials they've produced.

Chapter 5

TV to Retail—The REAL Road to Riches

For the first part of this book, we've focused on the huge profits to be made from DRTV ads. But there is a tendency for inventors or entrepreneurs to get tunnel vision about one profit stream or another. It's either TV or retail; retail or TV.

Might I suggest… *both*?

Now that you've recognized the massive potential a quality DRTV ad can have on your business plan, it's time to graduate to the next phase of launching your product to an entirely new "audience."

Or, as I like to call it: "TV to retail, the *real* road to riches."

The Road to Retail

The fact is that for every consumer that buys on TV, there are *5 to 10 that will never buy on TV.* Perhaps they have an aversion to commercials of all kinds, and automatically flip the channel the minute yours—or anyone's—comes on.

Maybe they've been burned by infomercials in the past and can't see through that experience to open their mind to yours. For whatever reason, the fact remains that there is a very specific, if high, ceiling on how many customers will actually purchase something they've seen "on TV"… from TV.

That doesn't mean that you can't make millions of dollars from TV infomercials alone, but… why stop there? Taking specific steps to merge your "As Seen on TV" product to retail shelves at the likes of Walgreens and Wal-Mart means that you can make much, much more when you go to retail.

If your true goal is to get your product seen, used and purchased by as many people as possible, TV can only take you so far. Resisting the urge to take your product from the airwaves to store shelves is almost like turning away money!

In a very real sense, too, if your ultimate goal IS to launch your new product in retail stores, more and more the only opportunity available to you is to produce a winning DRTV spot and produce impressive sales numbers in advance of pitching the product to retail.

Why? One simple reason: this reduces the risk for retailers.

Better Than Traditional Advertising?

Why the recent trend in seeing that instantly recognizable red "As Seen On TV" logo in some of today's most popular stores? The fact is, it's getting harder and harder for independent manufacturers, inventors and entrepreneurs to launch their products in retail first, and TV second. More and more often, the roles are reversed and inventors and entrepreneurs like you and me are seeing TV as the road to retail, and not the other way around.

Mass retailers like Wal-Mart, Target and Costco used to view infomercials as competition for the same consumer, but they now understand that infomercials *drive buyers into the stores* just as well as, if not better than, traditional advertising.

Gone is the "American dream" of pitching a new product, cold, to the powers that be at today's major retailers. Past performance, or the lack thereof, of one-off products from independent producers has all but closed the door to future opportunities for first-time product marketers.

Unfortunately, selling to mass retailers is becoming next to impossible for new companies with a single product. In fact, Wal-Mart recently instituted a new policy wherein they will not take in any new product from a new, single SKU vendor. Can you imagine? But look at the risk, and the reality, from inside their shoes. The risks are viewed as too great for the retailers to be the first ones to test a new product.

Why put all the money into advertising, shelf space, logistics, etc., if it's just going to fail? They'd rather invite a proven product to participate in their success than take the risk on an unproven product that will likely fail.

One great exception to this rule is "As Seen On TV" products. These products are growth engines for mass retailers, driving significant volume with significantly minimized risk.

Success is Repeatable

One reason retailers appreciate the validity of "As Seen On TV" products is that they have already been proven market leaders. After all, once a product has been successful on TV, it is a valuable proof of concept: it works, people like it, people need it, and people buy it. For companies who've been burned in the past by slick promises and lost opportunity, a successful ad and TV sales record makes it very likely that the product will also work in retail. For the retailers, it's repeatable success. It worked on TV, why wouldn't it work in our stores?

Consumers themselves feel the same way. Those who might not buy a product on TV for whatever reason might now see the product as more credible, more reliable, even more successful just because it's on the shelves at their favorite store.

Even the DRTV commercial itself is seen as a valid sales pitch. Right there in your two-minute, short-form TV spot or longer infomercial, the powers that be at Wal-Mart or Target, Walgreens or CVS can see how your product works, its value as compared to other similar products and, of course, its unique features and benefits (which is just one more reason to produce a really powerful DRTV spot!).

Today, As Seen On TV products are some of the most sought after products in retail. Consumers will often go into stores asking for your product when they see it on TV, which really helps the retail buyer to get into your corner quickly. Get your product to work on TV, and you'll likely get it to work in retail.

More Money, More Problems!

Be forewarned: retail can be much more complex to manage than direct-to-consumer sales. Remember how in addition to the production of your DRTV ad you need telemarketing, a website, inventory and shipping and handling? Well, add to that complexity with several additional major requirements and you'll get an idea of what it's like to transition from TV to retail.

Not to intimidate you, but here are some of the very real issues you'll need to face before a product is ready to fly off Wal-Mart's shelves:

- **Will you have enough inventory?** You need to pre-order large volumes of inventory. This may require a significant investment of time and money to ensure that you have enough to fulfill the huge demands if your product is wildly successful.

- **But not too much?** Conversely, you may risk inventory buybacks if your product doesn't sell well, even if it's the retailer's fault. Compliance is a huge issue at the retail level. Part of your agreement needs to be that retailers actually put the products on shelves, not let them sit in the back room gathering dust.
- **System integrity.** Your systems need to interface with the major retailers, so you will want to be aware of the specs of all of your retail outlets to ensure that there will be no costly "glitches" come launch time.
- **Potential fines.** Moving to retail means certain rules and regulations will need to be adhered to. In particular, you need to make sure your shipments are marked correctly, or you could face fines. For most retailers, fines are a profit center, so they are always looking for minor errors.
- **Bar coding.** How is your product bar-coded? Is it suitable for retail sale? Do you know?
- **Proper packaging requirements.** To comply with various retail outlets around the country, you will want to ensure that your product is packaged properly.
- **Have product, will travel.** In order to see your product successfully reach the sales floor, you will need to fly around the country to pitch your product face-to-face with dozens of key retailers.

Is it all worth it? Absolutely!

All that being said, the opportunity in retail is so great you cannot pass it up. Who will handle each of the bullet points above? Someone, somewhere, has the skill and ability.

For starters, don't reinvent the wheel, and don't try to do it all yourself. The profit potential of retail is such that it behooves you to hire experts who have done this before and let them tackle the various complexities.

Look for providers who have a proven track record in successfully launching retail products, and who keep close tabs to ensure that all projects are completed on time to avoid costly delays in launching the product in stores.

3 Options on Your Own Personal Road to Retail

What are your options to get your product in the aisles of your favorite grocery, drug or department store? Read further, and you might be surprised by how effective any or all of the following three strategies can be:

1.) **Hiring:** You have a product, you have a great DRTV ad and now retail wants to stock their shelves with your product. What to do? You don't need help with the product itself, or even the DRTV spot anymore. Your specific need is for someone to smooth the transition from direct shipping via call-in or web orders to an actual retail distribution model. One option is to hire an expert experienced in selling to retail channels to guide you through the strategy. Rather than employing a full-time person, this can be done as an outsourced consultant role.

2.) **Outsourcing:** Another option would be to outsource your retail fulfillment and systems compliance to one of many proven logistics companies.

3.) **Licensing:** License just the retail portion of your business to a major industry marketer that will handle all of the details. Many of the hottest products in Walgreens and Wal-Mart are marketed on TV by one company and distributed into retail by another company.

Parting Words about Retail

At the end of the day, the ultimate goal of any entrepreneurial exercise is to have a *product that people want*. Many people may want it via sale on TV; many more may want it off the retail shelves.

This chapter has hopefully shown you that if you think of DRTV as the beginning of your journey, then hopefully the finish line is a precious spot on one of those "As Seen on TV..." shelves in retail.

Chapter 6

Don't Forget About HSN/QVC (Hey, A Little More Revenue Never Hurt Anyone!)

Today we take for granted that you can sit in the comfort of your own home, watch glamorous hosts and hostesses—many of them celebrities like Joan Rivers or Suzanne Somers—sell affordable products, dial a simple 1-800 number, use your credit or debit card and receive the product in 3 to 5 days.

But once upon a time, there was no such thing as HSN, let alone QVC.

The Home Shopping Network (HSN) was the pioneer in the live television shopping industry that eventually spawned QVC and countless other international live television shopping networks that, today, sell billions of dollars' worth of merchandise every month.

Ordering products by phone was nothing new as early as the 1970s, when many of the DRTV pioneers got their start. Long before HSN (and, later, QVC), the Sell On TV "revolution" was limited to one-off infomercials or DRTV spots ala Ron Popeil's pocket fisherman or the Ch-Ch-Ch-Chia Pet.

While popular and ultimately successful as stand alone "commercials," there was no central station, let alone major network, devoted to "Order Now!" phone-in orders. Perhaps there didn't need to be. Sell On TV products had their place, for now, but all that was about to change in the late 70s and early 80s.

The Little Green Can Opener That Could: *From Humble Beginnings to Gold Standard Success*

HSN was founded in 1977 when an AM radio station owner (HSN founder and chairman, Roy Spear) had trouble collecting advertising receivables from a local electronics store. In exchange for (non) payment, Roy accepted 112 olive-green electric can openers and asked the show host, Bob Circosta, to sell the can openers during his show.

Even at $9.95 a piece, the can openers "sold out" and Spear and Circosta knew they were on to something! Circosta later became the new network's first ever 'home shopping host' and would eventually sell 75,000 different products in over 20,000 hours of live, on-air television.

HSN first aired as a local Tampa, Florida television station in the late-1980s—it was originally called the "Home Shopping Club"—and eventually moved to a 24-hour national cable network in the mid-1990s.

Today, HSN has revenues over $2.8 billion and Bob Circosta is still one of the most successful pitchmen on their network, and in the industry. We here at Harvest Growth are proud to be good friends with Bob. We work together to take many of his successful HSN products on to national TV infomercials and, eventually, into retail.

The Road to Riches: Another Path?

Now, why should you covet featured spots on HSN and/or QVC? For the same reason you vie for a precious spot on the retail store shelves; *increased profit stream*. In other words, we view the Home Shopping Network and QVC as *additional retailers*.

Once again, it all comes down to a successful DRTV production. Once your product is proven on TV, you can generally gain entry into HSN or QVC fairly easily. Why bother? The answer is simple: an appearance on one or the other network could easily add *$1 million*—or more—to your annual top line revenues.

How does it work? Basically, HSN or QVC will buy the product(s) wholesale from you and then pitch your product to a live audience. You can be on air with your product as often as once or twice per month. You can also hire a professional pitchperson ala Bob Circosta so you don't have to travel to their studios every airing.

These networks can also be a great predictor of success for your product before you produce your infomercial, but the process is long and slow if your product isn't proven, and the odds of getting on to the networks without proof of concept are slim.

Parting Words about HSN & QVC: What Does Success Look Like?

What can success on HSN or QVC look like? One great, recent example was the Bumpits line of hair volume products. Not only did the entire initial shipment of Bumpits sell out, but the product was then licensed to Allstar Marketing, a premier DRTV company. Today, total revenues are reputedly over $100 million!

Chapter 7

How to Manage Your Business So It Runs Itself

You've worked hard creating the product or invention you want to feature on TV, in retail and possibly even on HSN or QVC. To ensure that hard work wasn't for naught, it's important to have specific and achievable financial goals as a result.

One development that you want to understand early on is how to turn your product or invention into what's known as passive income. In other words, money that continues to accumulate "in your sleep."

Think about it; the success of a brand like the Pet Rock or OxiClean is that it is perpetual. Pet Rocks have been around for generations; long enough for grandparents to talk about them with their grandchildren—on an equal level.

Today the OxiClean brand is recognized worldwide and there are dozens of product offshoots all capitalizing on the same quality, effectiveness and consistency of the original, parent product. Chances are decades from now the builders of the Pet Rock and OxiClean empires will still be reaping the benefits that originated as a result of proper and timely TV ad placement.

Earn While You Toss and Turn

One of the beauties of DRTV is that the business earns money while you sleep. Once you've gone to the trouble, energy and upkeep of creating a successful product, then presented it properly on TV, it lives in perpetuity.

The reason so many actors, authors and musicians become millionaires is because of passive income in the form of residuals and royalties. Modern actors, especially those we consider "stars," are always participants in the profit-sharing created by their efforts.

That means every time an Ocean's 11 or a Mr. and Mrs. Smith runs on TV or is sold on DVD, Brad Pitt gets a cut. How small a cut is inconsequential when looked at in perspective. How many times does Mr. and Mrs. Smith or The River Runs Through It run on TNT or Fox every month? How many people pick them up for $10 or $20 or more at Wal-mart or Target every year?

Likewise, every time you download a Jay-Z album or, increasingly, a single song; "kaching," Mr. Z gets residuals. So does Paul McCartney, J-Lo, Janet Jackson or... Vanilla Ice! Stephen King has sold over 500 million books in his lifetime. Earning royalty rates on every book creates a "king-making" sum. It's also what's made Harry Potter author J. K. Rowling one of the richest authors on the planet!

Product marketing can work just as well. Like a book on Amazon.com or an album on iTunes, *media runs day and night*. It never sleeps, nor do many of your best customers! Consumers call into call centers or visit your product website 24 hours a day, 7 days a week, 365 days a year.

Old customers, new customers, a combination of both; referrals and link-throughs and merely the curious, they all contribute to bottom-line profit that runs all day, every day, as long as you want it to. All you have to do is sit back and reap the profits.

After the initial product testing and creation, it's all fulfillment and delivery. The products are packed and shipped by a third party fulfillment center (while you sleep). Then you check the reports weekly or so (when you're awake!).

If the business is stable, it practically runs itself. The key is selecting the right vendors. If you make a wrong choice, you may have a lot of headaches as you try to dig out of a hole. What's the solution? It's important to work with a trusted advisor that knows the industry and avoid common pitfalls.

Should I Do It Myself?

The question when it comes to bringing a product to the consumer market inevitably becomes, "Should I do it myself... or let someone else handle the responsibility for me?!?"

As someone who works with inventors and entrepreneurs all day long, I can tell you it's not a simple question to answer; nor one to take very lightly. Just as you can do some of the mock-ups and schematics for your product yourself, but leave the rest to others, you will want to consider—realistically—how much skill you'll need to create passive income from your DRTV launch.

Launching a consumer product can help you earn millions of dollars very quickly… but it can be a difficult task, especially if this is your first time treading these waters. If you consider all the "working pieces" of creating a cottage industry ala the Snuggie, Bumpits or OxiClean, you can get some kind of picture of the work that's cut out for you if you try to go it alone.

Some entrepreneurs and inventors approach Harvest Growth wondering if they will pay someone to launch their product or do it themselves. For some, the correct answer may be to at least start the launch process on their own, but for most, it makes sense to work with someone with years of experience.

Hiring outside expertise to guide you on your path to success helps you to avoid the common pitfalls that you're sure to encounter. Why repeat the mistakes of others if you don't have to?

"Going it alone" includes market research, inventing, designing, prototyping, patenting, sourcing, developing a website, producing a DRTV spot, developing the back-end business including telemarketing, fulfillment and payment processing, buying media, tracking performance, pitching to retailers and running the day-to-day business. The following matrix shows the many aspects that must be managed for a successful product launch.

SUCCESS FACTORS

Many entrepreneurs are proficient at the early stages of product development, but they require help taking their products to market. Know your strengths, and hire out the rest. A trusted and experienced adviser can fill in the gaps for an inventor and optimize the chances for success.

Another option is to license your product to a proven marketer that takes over all of the product development and day-to-day operations and pays you a royalty based on the success of your product.

We have found that the easiest and most profitable way to license your product is to perform a small test market to prove market demand. Once you have in-market results, licensees will compete against each other for your business.

Parting Words of Advice

In summary, it's your choice how involved you want to be in your product launch, but unless you are an experienced "marketeer," you'll ultimately save time and earn more money if you work with someone with deep-rooted experience in launching products. Consider leaving the complexities to someone else as you comfortably earn money in your sleep. Or learn from experts and go it alone for your second home-run product to further increase your profits.

Chapter 8

With a Great Idea, You Don't Need Money

Let's say you've got a great idea for a product but don't want to spend the money on a long- or even short-form DRTV ad, OR go to the trouble of shipping and distributing it yourself. However, like all great inventors you still want to cash in on the passive income your "great idea" can provide.

Does this mean you're stuck with a great idea—and nowhere to sell it?

Hardly. In fact, there is an option that can take your great idea and, with no money out of your pocket, put it to work for you so that you can still earn passive income. It's called *licensing*, and it's one more path you can take down the road to making money while you sleep.

When you take advantage of the lucrative licensing market, you can still make millions of dollars with your product—*even if you give up control to someone else*. Every year, hundreds of products are licensed to major DRTV companies, and inventors collect significant royalties from their sales.

If you think about it, licensing is a lot like publishing or making movies or the record business. When you write a book, you write it once and basically the publisher "licenses" it and sells it on your behalf.

You send it to the publisher as good as it can be, they polish it off for you, design a great cover, set up all the distribution channels, get it up on Amazon.com, do some marketing, ship it to the bookstores and... instant passive income. The author receives royalties on each book sold, probably while still writing his next one.

The same is true with record labels or movie studios. Once a musician or actor has done his or her creative best, the record label or studio then sends that "product" out into the open market, generating income for both themselves and the artist, who also get "royalties," in the music industry, or "residuals" in the motion picture world.

Or imagine your favorite superhero, like Spiderman, Batman or Iron Man. All a cartoonist has to do is create one hit comic book, and if it's a big enough hit—or even has the potential to be one—everyone from T-shirt manufacturers to toy companies will want to "license" that hero and put his or her face on a variety of products, each one of them earning that cartoonist money while he or she sleeps.

Like all business partnerships where one side (the inventor) is basically "creative" and the other does most of the "heavy lifting" (the licensee) or, in this case, the advertising, shipping, handling, distribution, returns, etc., the split is rarely ever "even."

Generally, if you choose to go this route and license your product, you can expect royalty rates from between 1 percent of revenues to 8 percent of revenues. The range is driven by a variety of factors, of course, to include:

- **Which company is doing the licensing?**
- **Is your product patented?**
- **Is it proven in market?**
- **Do you have a prototype or fully manufactured units?**
- **What is the margin for the product?**
- **Do you have a relationship with any of the top-tier licensees?**
- **Etc.**

While the prospect of "handing over" your product can seem attractive, particularly when eyeing those potential millions, *be careful*. For every trusted licensee, there are dozens that have reputations for ripping off the inventors.

However, with that said, many are very trustworthy, and if you don't want to stay involved in the business or don't have the financing to get started, licensing can be a great way to make a lot of money—even millions of dollars!—without a lot of effort.

Chapter 9

Free Advertising!
How Even Billion Dollar Brands Are Starting to Use Infomercial Marketing

Once upon a time, "infomercials" were reserved for a very specific breed of product, best seen on TV and, preferably, late at night. In the pioneering days of Mr. Microphone and the Ginsu knife, the infomercial market was sparsely populated and those products that did air on TV had unlimited "shelf space," so to speak.

Those were the days...

Today, of course, it seems as if everyone is entering the DRTV space, even so-called "traditional" brand names who as little as two or three years ago might not have even considered selling their products direct-to-consumer.

In 2010, for instance, fast food behemoth Taco Bell produced a 30-minute infomercial highlighting their "Drive Thru Diet." They spent millions in advertising driving their brand, as well as a new concept for them: losing weight through fast-food. Clearly the powers that be at Taco Bell realized the power and impact of the long-form TV marketing method and decided to tap into this most powerful of tools.

Imagine the freedom the marketing department must have felt to be able to share their message in 30-minutes versus the traditional 30-second TV spot. The long format allowed them to truly hammer home the larger message that Taco Bell cares about its customers and their healthcare needs.

The DRTV format was a great way for them to share a new idea through a new medium. And while TV is hardly new to Taco Bell, the creator of some of TV's edgiest and most celebrity-driven advertising, having the freedom to fill 30-minutes was the right decision for the right message at the right time. The message is clear: if the DRTV model works for big, billion-dollar companies, it can work for you as well.

I like to tell my clients that the world of "As Seen on TV" has grown up and companies like Taco Bell and, before them, industry giants like Proactiv and OxiClean have given respectability to a once admittedly laughable late-night TV landscape. Gone are the days that shady purveyors of questionable goods are crowding the airwaves. Production quality has gone way up, and DRTV is now a trusted medium in consumers' minds. In other words, they are no longer ashamed of what they order on TV and, in fact, will loudly proclaim a great find to friends and families alike.

Huge brands....real brands....have built credible empires with the DRTV model. Who, exactly? The DRTV success stories read like a "Who's Who" of industry elite:

- **Proactiv (over $500 million in annual revenues)**
- **OxiClean (in over 50,000 retail stores)**
- **Trojan Condoms (now using DRTV advertising as one of its major marketing vehicles)**
- **Proctor & Gamble (Mr. Clean and others)**
- **even Kraft Foods (Gevalia Coffee)**

The household names above—and many more—are all using DRTV to drive their brands... and so can you. DRTV is powerful for big brands and brand new products because it can give you *free advertising*.

How is a $50,000 or $60,000 buy-in "free"? Think of how quickly you can earn that money back with one big shipment of product, with one appearance on HSN or QVC. And through DRTV, you can actually *earn money from your advertising*. That way, you increase your spend as high as you can until the returns start to decline, thus maximizing awareness to drive sales in multiple channels.

DRTV for Less: Save on Media Costs, No Matter Your Product.

Did you know that "regular advertisers" can save up to 70 percent off their television media rates just by adding a simple URL to their ad? Many big advertisers shy away from direct-response advertising because they don't want to tarnish their brand with hard-hitting advertising ala Billy Mays. However, oftentimes, all it takes to qualify for the discounted rates is the addition of a URL to your ad. Remnant, or discounted, media is available on virtually all national cable television stations, and you can purchase time with 30-second and 15-second ads.

How Can You Measure Success?

Another benefit of direct-response media is measurability. The reps at the big ad agencies don't want you to know about this, as it is true accountability; something they have a hard time offering their deep-pocketed clientele.

How do you know if a five- or even six-figure social media campaign is working? Facebook friends and Twitter followers don't all mean actual customers, and measurement can be hard to come by with traditional media as well.

Harvest Growth has worked with the biggest agencies while managing brands for Kraft Foods, Schick and others, so we've seen firsthand the lack of measurement offered by most of them.

The "flash" may be missing from the DR media agencies, but they offer *real_results* and, what's more, *real accountability*. In my opinion it's important to find where your consumers are through direct-response media rather than taking educated guesses with traditional media.

Chapter 10

Increase Your Odds of Success with Market Research

If you launch it, will they buy?

That's the question every inventor wants to know, but unfortunately there is no crystal ball where you can easily find the answer. Instead, we have something known as "market research," where rather than reading tea leaves and consulting a psychic, you put hard evidence together with profit projections to get a firm answer.

So, before you commit to launching your product, you will want to do two things:

1. **Make sure people will buy it, and...**
2. **Make sure you are able to communicate the product's benefits clearly and concisely.**

Both of these vital pieces of knowledge can be gained with *market research*, in general, and in *focus groups* and *surveys* in particular:

Focus on Focus Groups

The use of "focus groups" is known as qualitative research and is comprised of groups of 6 to 12 people in a room that fit your demographic. Friends and family are acceptable, but it's best to recruit people that *don't know you* when you get serious about your research so your relationship with them doesn't bias their comments.

What you don't want in a focus group is a bunch of "yes" men and women who will tell you what they think you want to hear because they care about you. What you want are folks who will give you the "straight scoop," even if it stings a little. If you trust your friends and family to be objective and honest, by all means they can participate.

How will you run your focus group? Well, you can either hire a professional moderator for a total cost of $5,000 to $8,000 per group or attempt to do your own focus group—for less than half that cost. The choice really depends on your comfort level and your ability to objectively ask questions.

Remember, the goal of this exercise is twofold:

1. **Make sure people will buy your product, and…**
2. **Make sure you are able to communicate the product's benefits clearly and concisely.**

Focus groups are great for getting answers on the creative aspect of your product and on drilling deeper to explore its features and benefits. Asking the right types of questions will provide honest answers, not just positive ones.

Focus groups can be an extremely effective market research tool to help understand consumers' perceptions of a product. Like any market research, there is a time and a place for focus groups, and they are certainly not the end-all-be-all tool.

However, we at Harvest Growth have found them to be extremely helpful when writing an infomercial script. In small group settings, consumers share their feelings and opinions in ways that can't be communicated in surveys.

After all, here is a chance to have up to a dozen potential consumers interact in a casual, comfortable small group setting. It's like being able to talk to customers face to face and ask them questions no survey could recreate.

Body language is powerful. Don't just listen to what participants have to say, but watch when they answer a question or join a discussion. Are they scowling even as they praise you? Are they shaking their heads when they're saying "yes"? When their expressions don't match their words, it's time to probe deeper!

3 Secrets to Effective Focus Groups

At Harvest Growth, we use focus groups most frequently to review advertising creative concepts, infomercial scripts and also as a "gut check" for products we are considering for our portfolio.

In the past 10+ years, I have facilitated or attended well over 100 focus groups, and have learned several secrets that can be applied to almost any group.

Here are three of our favorites:

The First Secret: Thumbs Up-Thumbs Down

One of the hazards in a focus group is that consumers will influence each other. It's just human nature. One member of the group feels strongly about a certain aspect, vocalizes his concerns and, through force of will or personality, influences the group until even those who don't necessarily agree with him are subconsciously on his "side."

One of the most effective ways of minimizing the dangers of this type of "groupthink" is to force focus group participants to make quick judgments. Rather than idly taking their time and giving in to their groupthink urges, forcing quick answers will help group participants react personally rather than communally.

We like to use the "thumbs up / thumbs down" method of forcing a vote. In this scenario, there is no gray area. You either agree or disagree. We ask a question, and participants respond—quickly—with a thumbs up (for "yes") or thumbs down (for "no"). You either like the product, or you don't. Once these quick judgments are made, participants feel more comfortable as they share their other opinions.

The Second Secret: Write Down Your Answers

Similar to "thumbs up / thumbs down," when we ask participants to write down their answers, they are forced to share their opinion with zero influence from others in the group. They are allowed to elaborate without the peer pressure or "groupthink" of others, and this way can respond honestly and without censor.

This technique is particularly useful when we ask open-ended questions like:

- "How much would you be willing to pay for this product?"
- "What do you like most about this product?"

- **""Where would you expect to find this product?"**
- **Etc.**

The Third Secret: Circle Your Favorite(s) and Cross Out Your Least Favorite(s)

Before producing an infomercial for a first-time client, Harvest Growth always runs a consumer focus group to help with the creative development. Consumers aren't particularly valuable as tools to help write a script from scratch, but they are invaluable when it comes to helping decide the focus of the infomercial.

If you try to write a script in-house, with just you and a creative team who does this for a living, it's very easy to focus on the features and benefits that matter most to you, rather than the actual consumer. Focus groups allow you to shift the "focus" back to them, which is obviously very valuable in terms of objective, uncensored feedback.

Our favorite technique for creative review is to write down 20+ "scriptlets" that are quick phrases that might be heard in an infomercial, such as "For a limited time only" or "Act now and get twice the offer" or even "Order in the next 30 seconds and get...", but tailored to the specifics of the product being marketed. We also write out the key features and benefits separately.

We ask participants to review the entire list, circle their favorites and cross out their least favorites. One mistake made by many advertising producers is writing the script "in a vacuum," so to speak, without active audience or focus group participation.

This results in a script that excites the producer and the creative team, but has no consumer relevance whatsoever. Have you ever watched a movie and found yourself disinterested and uninvolved, scratching your head at all the inside jokes and wondering why the actors looked like they were having so much fun? Chances are, they made the movie for themselves—and nobody else!

Infomercials are no different; don't just make one for yourself! Involving consumers early in the creative process can make a monstrous difference in the performance of an infomercial, thus saving tens of thousands of dollars in testing and refinement.

You might be asking yourself right about now, "If it's so important to not have participants influence each other, why don't you just interview them one-on-one?" Our secrets to effective focus groups are intended to overcome the natural tendency for people to want to talk and to combine their opinions with one another.

Then, too, there is inherent value in collective feedback. In fact, for 90 percent of the questions we ask any focus group, this interaction among members of the group is actually ideal. We *want* them to feed off of each other as we discuss features, benefits, personal experiences with the product category and more.

For questions like pricing, likes/dislikes and "favorites" from a list of choices, it's important to make sure the opinions are true, unbiased, non-influenced opinions. As we counsel in the beginning of all our focus groups, "We only want to hear YOUR opinion, not your neighbor's, your dad's, or even your husband's opinion."

To that end, the leader/facilitator of the focus group plays an integral part in remaining a proactive leader but not an influencing presence. The last thing you want to do is have a group influenced by a company representative, or even an outside facilitator.

And the Survey Says…

Surveys are what are known as quantitative research. Unlike focus groups, surveys are handled remotely and without any personal interaction whatsoever. In the ideal scenario, you carefully craft a survey of between 10 and a 50 questions and send to 100 or more people. Why so many? To a certain extent, the more people that participate in a survey, the more realistic and representative the results tend to be. Sending a survey to five people produces results that are hard to extrapolate across the wider spectrum.

For instance, let's say all five of the respondents were from… a nursing home. Chances are, the information will be very similar. Sending to at least 100 people allows you the opportunity to reach a wider, more varied audience.

Regardless of the size or scope of the audience, everyone who receives the survey is asked the same questions so you can tabulate the answers. "83 percent believe this product solves a common, everyday problem…"

Quantitative research is great for answering pricing questions, for comparing multiple products and for answering what we call Purchase Intent. In other words, what percentage of people are interested in purchasing your product.

What's involved in producing a survey? Surveys generally cost over $10,000 when performed by an outside agency, but can be free if you use one of several internet sites like www.SurveyMonkey.com. Generally, you'll need to provide or purchase the respondent list, but this is a much cheaper alternative than laying out 10 grand for the privilege.

Parting Words about Market Research: Keep an Open Mind

Regardless of whether you use a focus group, a survey or both, the key to gathering good market research is to keep an open mind. Oftentimes we have an ideal picture in our mind, not just of how our product will perform but how it will perform on the market.

Market research allows us to get an objective view of our own product and how actual customers, in the form of focus groups or surveys, actually feel about it. Sometimes the answers may surprise you, but rest assured no one is out to hurt your feelings or derail your dreams!

Instead, keep an open mind and keep doing market research. If you keep getting the same feedback in a variety of forms, from a variety of people from all walks of life, chances are it's valid and worth acting on. But it's better to know it now, before your product launch, than after!

Chapter 11

Test, Test, Test

Every day at Harvest Growth we receive several excited phones calls and emails from first-time inventors that believe they have created "the next big thing." While their inventions may range from hair care products to high-tech gadgets, their pitch seldom varies:

- *"This is an incredible idea that has **never been tried before.**"*
- *"If I could just show the product to consumers, **I know** they would buy it."*
- ***"Price isn't an issue** for something this special; people will pay whatever I ask."*
- *"I have dozens of other compelling products up my sleeve **if we can make this one work**..."*
- *"Did we mention **no one has ever seen anything like this? EVER!?!?**"*

Don't get me wrong; we absolutely *love* working with inventors; they are the lifeblood not just of our business, but of the entrepreneurial spirit that dominates this great country. And we firmly believe that "the next big thing" could very well be their product.

I mean, who are we to pass judgment on the next Bumpit, OxiClean, ShamWow, Ginsu knife or Snuggie? And, frankly, that's what we most love about our jobs: every day we wake up wondering, "What sort of great ideas will we hear today?"

Is this the day we stumble across the next Ped Egg?

Pocket Fisherman?

Pillow Pets!?!?

The fact is, all great products start with a great pitch. But promises aren't what get me hot under the collar for a new product, invention or idea; *results do*. Don't tell me what you think; tell me what you know! "But," you ask, "how does a new inventor get results to prove that his or her product really IS the next big thing?"

The answer is simple: test it.

Then test it some more...

Test, Test and Test Some More!

No matter how good your idea is, testing should be a vital part of your marketing ramp-up. The good news is, you're halfway there. That's because direct-response television marketing is an ideal vehicle for performing in-market tests with relatively minimal upfront expense.

There are several elements of your campaign that you absolutely should test, and a few that probably aren't worth the time or money; we'll cover them both. For now, the following variables can dramatically impact your results. (Case in point: we've seen some subtle changes in the below factors improve results by up to 500 percent!):

Price Point

When it comes to price point, i.e. what you charge the consumer, more is not always better. In fact, sometimes less really IS more; more sales, that is. The simple philosophy is that the higher you charge per sale, the more each sale will be worth. That way, you can actually sell less and still make more.

Likewise, there are those who believe that if you charge as little as possible you will sell so much more that it will even surpass the higher price point. This isn't always ideal either. And that's what we're looking for here: the ideal. Or, as it's called in our industry, the *optimal price point*.

The goal is to be a little like Goldilocks; not too hot, not too cold, not too big, not too small, but just right. In our world, "just right" is the optimal price you should be charging for the product you're offering.

Now, we know perfectly well that you might already be successfully selling your item to a few boutique retailers for $30 or $40, but you might be able to quadruple your revenues—AND your profits—by finding the optimal price point, normally $10.00, $14.99 or $19.99 for a two-minute DRTV spot.

While it may seem like a big leap to come down $20 or even $30 in price, testing will prove out how you can actually make more—in many cases significantly more—by actually charging less.

Additionally, your production costs may currently be too high to be able to sell for $19.99 or less, but you need to plan your costs around high sales and production volumes rather than around short-term, low quantity "test" production runs.

Offer

The offer is different than the "price point." The offer includes the structure of *how you are selling the price point*. "Buy One, Get One" (BOGO) and "buy our main product, and we'll give you this premium product FREE!" are two of the proven examples of great offers that work effectively over time.

Which offer will work best for you? There's no way to know until you begin testing to find just the right offer for your product.

Upsells

Have you ever bought a basic cell phone for a "one time, all-time low price" of $19.99, only to walk out with an additional $80 worth of charger cables, battery packs, phone cases, belt hooks and a wireless headset? If so, welcome to the wonderful world of upsells!

In other words, what are you selling AFTER the consumer picks up the phone or visits your website to place an order for what they actually saw on TV? We have helped $19.99 products have an average order value as high as $70 once the upsells are included. Choosing the right upsells can make the difference between a "monster hit" and a "bomb."

Various upsells for a variety of products include:

- **A premium shampoo or conditioner to go with their Bumpit**
- **Patented rubber gloves and portable stain-remover sticks to go with their tub of OxiClean**
- **A "grooming kit" to keep their Homer Simpson Chia Pet from looking unruly**

- A knife block, lifetime guarantee sharpening blade and set of steak knives to accompany their original Ginsu knife
- Etc.

Creative

Are you selling the right features and benefits for the right product at the right time? We've been hired for several projects where we were asked to "fix" the campaign after the original commercial missed the mark.

We firmly believe in performing consumer research BEFORE you write the script for your DRTV commercial to make sure the benefits are compelling to consumers before time and effort go into filming something that may land with a thud instead of a round of applause.

Two minutes of television advertising sounds like a lot of time to push, promote and sell your product, but if you don't focus on the correct key messaging, it can easily go to waste and leave viewers far from impressed. The creative has to drastically change from the control version in order to have a significant impact.

What "creative" elements am I talking about? Here are just a few:

- **Visuals:** Visuals are the tiny details that help make a blah TV ad sing. The credit card you use to show how small a restaurant magnifying glass can be, the hearing aid that lets you hear through walls; these are all great visuals that help solidify the product in the viewer's minds.
- **Talent:** Who will ever forget Billy Mays or, for that matter, Vince Shlomi, best known as the "ShamWow" guy? Hosts like those two are hard to forget, and tend to get the viewing audience as excited about the product—any product—as the hosts are!
- **Backdrop:** What setting have you proposed as the backdrop of your DRTV ad? If it's something active, like a toy or pair of sunglasses or even a hearing aid, take it outdoors. Don't depict an active product in a static environment. In other words, if you have a hose attachment that can reach three stories off the ground, show it in action! If you have

sunglasses that block out 20 percent more UV rays than the average pair, show people wearing it on a sunny day doing outdoorsy things.

- **Demonstration:** Put the product to good use. If it's a hair care product, for instance, show the typical female using it, then a younger female, then an older female. Show how easy it is to use at home in front of the vanity, at work in the employee locker room or even in the front seat of your car before a big meeting! For many products, the demonstration—or "demo"—can turn a losing product into a home run. OxiClean wasn't the first oxidizing cleaner on the market, and certainly wasn't the first stain remover. What separated OxiClean from the herd was, in part, Billy Mays as talent. But even with all that talent, what people *first* remembered from the original infomercial was his "fishbowl demo," where Billy magically turned black water to clear with small scoop of OxiClean. This type of "torture demo" proves that your product solves not only the everyday problem, but also the toughest problem you could possibly encounter. The "fishbowl demo" built credibility and excitement.

When Testing Becomes Counterproductive

Not all tests are created equal. In fact, some variables are probably not worth your time or money:

"Groundbreaking Creative"

When can the creative get too creative? When you try to be groundbreaking in a format that is very tried and true and has provided predictable results for hundreds and hundreds of products over several decades' time.

Unfortunately, we have worked with several clients that wish to "reinvent the wheel," so to speak, and turn creative into "groundbreaking." The results are often disastrous.

While it's true that the tone of the creative can stray from the traditional and still work, there are a few variables that you just don't change when you are testing a new product. There are very few, if any, examples of DRTV spots that diverted from the proven path and still achieved profitable results.

There are many examples, however, that grab your attention in a new way (such as Bumpits), introduce a talent that you just can't turn away from (ShamWow's Vince Shlomi) or completely avoided their true benefit for legal reasons (Extenze... probably not repeatable for other categories), BUT none of these diverted from the proven principles of DRTV. They all created an immense value and a strong sense of urgency to compel you to "call now."

Also, they were all very effective at communicating features and benefits. And, ultimately, that's the goal: to sell the product. If you want to be "groundbreaking-ly" creative with your TV spots, you may belong in Hollywood—not in retail. The time for testing "fun" creative that will "shake up the DRTV industry" is AFTER you've proven that your product can work on TV.

Idea Village did a masterful job at this with their MicroTouch army campaign. (You may remember the small shaving device being discussed during basic training, "can it shave even a private's privates?") However, they only pulled it off after spending millions of dollars growing their brand with traditional DRTV advertising first.

Hard to Predict New Product Success

"90 percent of new products fail!"

I've heard that mantra time and time again. As an entrepreneur, you'll hear similar negative discouragements from your friends and family as you take "crazy risks" to go out on your own to realize your dreams.

The sad fact is, that statement is partially true. Actually, when all product launches are considered, much more than 90 percent of new products fail. Even at the biggest and best consumer products companies in the world, they only succeed with a big winner less than 10 percent of the time. I saw this truism in action when I managed new product launches at Kraft Foods, and the same stat is true for the biggest DRTV product marketers as well. Imagine, if even 90 percent of a company like Kraft's initiatives fail how important market research and product testing is for the rest of us!

Clearly, such statistics indicate how hard it is to predict what will work and what won't. The reason we love direct-response marketing is that the cost to test launch your product is low, and you know very quickly whether or not your product is going to be a "hit" with consumers.

Traditional consumer products firms will spend between $2MM and $10MM on a product launch BEFORE they know if it will be successful or not. For DRTV firms, that number can be as low as $50k.

At such a low test market cost, there is no reason to not "test your dream." Likewise, if you're serious about testing, keep an open mind. There is no reason to spend $50k and then "pooh, pooh" the results because they don't automatically align with your preconceived notions.

So if you have a product idea that you've been eagerly working on for months or years, test it. Take it to market. The only way to see if consumers will like it as much as you—and your creative team—do is to put it out there and see the response. Market research is helpful, and certainly serves a purpose, but eventually, you need to pull the trigger and try to sell your product.

That's where testing—and lots of it—comes in…

Parting Words about Testing

When you're ready to go to market, work with a mentor that has done it before. Testing takes time, talent and experience. Knowing what to test, and when, and how often, and what for can save countless mistakes from trial and error down the road, and ensure that you have a hit your first time out to market—and not on your tenthth try. Remember, if "only" 90 percent of new products fail each year, that means a whopping 10 percent succeed. Why can't that be you?

Just as importantly, why go it alone? When you work with an experienced partner, your odds of success go way up. Test! But test wisely, and you'll improve the odds of your product becoming "the next OxiClean."

Chapter 12

Patents, Trademarks and Contract Review

No book on introducing a modern product to the open market today would be complete without a chapter on patents, trademarks and contract review. These days, there are simply too many ways to protect yourself—and we all need protection—to avoid the topic. (Still, I'll try to make it as painless as possible.)

Patents, Problems and Procrastination

When you mention to anyone that you're inventing something new, producing a new product or about to "go to market," one of the first thing folks will tell you is that you "need a patent."

We say: maybe, maybe not. How does a patent protect you? According to the United States Patent and Trademark Office, "A patent for an invention is the grant of a property right to the inventor, issued by the Patent and Trademark Office. The term of a new patent is 20 years from the date on which the application for the patent was filed in the United States."

In short, a patent protects you from others infringing on your product by granting you "the right to exclude others from making, using, offering for sale, or selling" the invention in the United States or 'importing' the invention into the United States." [**Source:** www.uspto.gov]

We are often asked the question, "Does my product need a patent?"

The answer is, "Well… it depends."

This is a tough question to answer in a book because the needs of every product are different. If we could see the product, hold it, view its specs, we could give a more definitive answer, but even then there is no "one size fits all" response.

So what *do* we suggest when it comes to patents? We would generally refer you to a trained patent attorney to get the best advice. However, that being said, most products that are launched via DRTV are *not patented*.

Why? Well, for one reason, patents are expensive. How expensive? Generally speaking, you're looking at an out of pocket cost of more than $10,000 just to get started. But that's not all; they can take years to issue. In the meantime, competitors are *always* looking for ways around your patent.

While here at Harvest Growth we're definitely in favor of protecting yourself, at the same time we are firm believers that *speed to market* is generally the most powerful protection.

In that case, DRTV helps you ramp up your spending, your revenues and your awareness very quickly so that it's difficult to copy you fast enough to beat you to market and, by the time a competitor does finally make it to market, they are in a distant second place.

Remember, the product is only part of what you have to offer. Service, reliability, quality, attention to detail, marketing and dominating the market as a brand will help make you a standout regardless of how many competitors follow in your path.

While a cheap knockoff might dilute your profits for a quarter or two, consumers will quickly recognize that saving a few bucks isn't worth being without what you and your product has to offer. Meanwhile, being second to market in DRTV is the kiss of death. Very few products succeed if they're not first out of the gate.

Possibly the best case study proving this theory is OxiClean. It didn't take long for large consumer products companies to take notice when OxiClean started selling millions of units and stealing market share from Clorox, Procter & Gamble, S.C. Johnson, Reckitt Benckiser and other multi-billion dollar consumer products companies with major laundry products. OxiClean generated tens of millions of dollars of sales on HSN and via DRTV, and as soon as OxiClean moved into mass retailers like Wal-Mart, Target and grocery stores, the big competitors developed copycat products.

Clorox's OxyMagic was perhaps the biggest threat. OxiClean's sales levels declined for a year or two as Clorox invested heavily behind this new brand. However, in the long run, OxiClean remained a powerhouse brand and OxyMagic lost distribution and became a "B player." Today, OxiClean is the number one stain removal product on the market, even though the formula can be easily copied, and patent and trademark protection is relatively week. Success was built on the backs of rapid awareness and distribution growth.

So, when are patents appropriate? In our opinion, patents become much more important if you are looking to license your product to another company. It will increase the value of your product and generally get you a higher royalty rate.

Talking About Trademarks

If patents are optional, then our advice on trademarks is much more direct: *trademarks are crucial*! Where patents are intended to protect your product from being copied, trademarks protect your *brand name* from being copied.

Says the United States Patent and Trademark Office, "A trademark is a word, name, symbol or device which is used in trade with goods to indicate the source of the goods and to distinguish them from the goods of others."

This type of legal protection from infringement is essential in this day and age. Now more than ever, trademarks are especially valuable on the Internet. Without trademark protection, competitors will use your trademark as a search term online and steal your customers.

Consider the "for Dummies" guides; "for Dummies" is trademarked and now prevents others from siphoning off the Dummies guides' promotion, marketing and publishing efforts by simply labeling their book, *"Fill in the blank* for Dummies." Other popular trademarks include Coca-Cola's "It's the Real Thing" and Maxwell House's "Good to the Last Drop."

So let's say you're a new company and you've worked hard to brand yourself in a way that is unique and individual to you and your new product. Maybe you come up with a cute slogan for your one-of-a-kind heated gardening pad that goes something like, "So warm, it'll bring you to your knees."

If you don't trademark this slogan, anyone can use it. Which means if your product blows up and people begin to associate your slogan with you, others can profit off of all your hard work by merely using the slogan for any old thing; not only building their brand on your shoulders but diluting your brand in the process.

Perhaps more important is the trademarking of your brand name itself. Although you have some protection inherently just by taking your product to market, we strongly recommend that you trademark your brand name to keep away copycats as far away from your product positioning as possible.

Clearly this protection is invaluable, now more than ever, but it's also inexpensive. How inexpensive? You can get trademark protection for under $1,000, including attorney fees. We recommend using an experienced trademark attorney to answer and explain all your specific questions, but you can also use inexpensive website services like www.legalzoom.com.

Contract Review

One thing about launching a new product: there is a LOT of paperwork involved. Contracts for this company, contracts for that. Every vendor you use, every company you do business with, every hand that touches your product will require a legal and binding contract.

Who will review them to make sure your best interest is at the forefront of any signed document? It's worth the expense to have an attorney review your license agreement and other vendor contracts.

While it may seem like a hassle, the very process of a formal contract review is there to make sure that you are getting exactly what you're expecting—and not the other way around. Once you find a trusted attorney, a quick contract review will generally cost a few hundred dollars at the most. If you can't find a good attorney on your own, you can call our offices and ask for recommendations. We work with several attorneys that are very experienced in reviewing DRTV industry contracts, thus reducing the costs even further. However, when possible, it's generally best to find a good attorney in your own community that you can develop a relationship with so they can act as a trusted advisor on other future business issues.

Parting Words about Patents, Trademarks and Contract Review

Inventing something new, creating a new product and bringing it to the American retail marketplace is the dream of many a modern entrepreneur. What most people don't realize about achieving their dreams is that one day they might just become a reality.

The "reality" of modern life is that, whether consciously or unconsciously, people often "borrow" ideas rather than create their own. That is why patents, trademarks and even things like contract review are in so important. You have worked hard to create something valuable and unique to yourself; now all you have to do is just work a little bit harder to protect it!

Chapter 13

The History of Infomercials, Or: Growing from the Basement to the Penthouse

While infomercials and Big Brother might seem to have nothing in common, the fact of the matter is that the history of infomercials received a huge shot in the arm because of a kind of "perfect storm" of government supervision—or, in this case, the lack thereof.

Case in point: in 1984, Congress enacted the Cable Communications Policy Act, which deregulated cable television. Subsequently, the Cable Franchise Policy and Communications Act was signed, and it no longer allowed cable operators to have editorial control over programming.

The "sea change" in cable TV allowed creative and fast-thinking marketers to take advantage of an unprecedented "block" of formerly inaccessible air time. To fill advertising gaps, initially in the middle of the night when most stations historically went dark, consumer product marketers bought this airtime inexpensively, and started selling products directly to consumers.

The Wild West of Late Night Infomercials

The early DRTV formats were initially almost entirely 30 minute infomercials purchased for extremely low airtime rates. Imagine huge swaths of late-night programming suddenly up for grabs at dirt cheap prices and you'll get a feel for what the "wild west" of early infomercial programming must have felt like.

Long before cable stations ran re-runs of their prime-time programming or all-night sci-fi movie marathons, infomercials became more than mere "commercials"; they became the only "entertainment" available on television in the middle of the night in many areas.

The groundbreakers of early infomercial history read like a Who's Who of the celebrity, the entrepreneurial, the smart, the shrewd, the famous and the infamous. Early pioneers included Jane Fonda selling exercise videos, Ginsu knives slicing through beer cans and the ubiquitous Ron Popeil selling myriad kitchen gadgets.

Psychic networks. Real Estate Millions. Self Help. These were the early successes, and the categories still thrive today, although Real Estate has transformed to Internet Millions and psychic networks have morphed to chat lines. Gone are the days of the humble, the unappreciated and the "fringe" products shilling on late-night TV. Today's "infomercial land" is filled with the famous, the big brands and the celebrities. Self Help is still ruled by the likes of Anthony Robbins, while infomercial products like the George Foreman Grill, the ThighMaster, OxiClean and Proactiv have become household names unto themselves.

Of course, those in the infomercial industry weren't exactly forthcoming about their secret to instant TV success. At first, millions of dollars were being made by only a select few. Today, of course, the infomercial industry boasts revenues over $150 billion, and hundreds of marketers are participating in this high-profit industry.

Spend an evening watching infomercials closely and you're likely to see products pitched by folks just like you; entrepreneurs, inventors and pioneers with a great idea and the resources to put it on the air. Some of them do it themselves; most of them partner with experienced marketing firms to see their DRTV dreams come true. Either way, the sky is the limit in this limitless and repeatedly groundbreaking industry.

TV to Retail: The Ultimate Opportunity

Telebrands is considered a pioneer of the short-form direct-response marketing world. Telebrands founder AJ Khubani moved his consumer products company into DRTV in 1987, when the modern infomercial industry was still in its infancy.

In his first year, he produced three short-form commercials that you're sure to recognize: Easy Cycle, the Ultrasonic Flea Collar and AmberVision Sunglasses. While all were game-changers for Telebrands, AmberVision was perhaps its biggest success, eventually selling over 15 million pairs and setting the foundation for this pioneer company to remain a leader in the DRTV industry for decades to come.

AJ quickly saw the potential of retail, and he began copying competitors' products that were already successful on TV and taking them into retail. While it may seem like a no-brainer now, this is nearly impossible to do today because all marketers now realize that retail is the *ultimate opportunity*, and they begin pitching their own products to retailers as soon as they see some success on TV.

Today, Telebrands is still selling hundreds of millions of dollars' worth of products on TV. Some recent successes have been the Windshield Wonder, the Ped Egg, the Stick Up Bulb and many more.

Ever been able to tell a product you've "seen on TV" before, even from a dozen paces, thanks to that big, bright red and white TV screen logo? Well, you have AJ and his creative team to thank for that! That's because Telebrands also developed the now infamous "As Seen On TV" logo that is on every retail package of nearly all products sold via TV infomercials. The logo itself is not trademarked, so dozens, if not hundreds of companies use a similar logo device on their retail packaging to bring credibility and to draw attention to their product.

AJ's two brothers are also marketing masters in their own right and are following in the DRTV tradition and promoting products you're sure to recognize. Chuck Khubani owns OnTel Products (the creators of Swivel Sweeper, Iron Gym, etc.) and Andy Khubani owns Idea Village (the mind behind HD Vision Sunglasses, Smooth Away, etc.) If you think there isn't enough room on TV to spread around, think again: Both brothers own $100 million plus competitive businesses.

Allstar Marketing is another $100 million plus business that tests products on television first and quickly moves to retail. Big successes for Allstar have been the Snuggie, Topsy Turvy Tomato Planter, BumpIts, Bendaroos and more.

Defying the Trends: The OxiClean Story, Take Two!

OxiClean was the first major direct-response television product to truly take advantage of mass retail in a way that could have staying power. Historically (or as I like to tell my clients, B.O.C., or Before OxiClean!), As Seen On TV products only had a lifespan of 1 to 3 years.

Gadgets and gizmos were sold to the masses, often in tens of millions of units, but they quickly saturated the markets and were soon taken off store shelves as the marketing companies went back to pursue the "next big hit." It was an endless cycle that fed upon itself but also was victim to the whims and fads of the buying public, as well as the faddish nature of the products themselves.

Along came OxiClean! OxiClean developed a product that was perfect for retail. There was nothing faddish or overexposed about it. Here was a stain remover that every home in America could use and, best of all, one that needed to be replenished every couple of weeks. Brilliant!

Your Time is NOW: Join the Fray!

And now it's your turn.

History is being made as we speak, not just by Fortune 500 companies with established products, distribution channels and million dollar advertising campaigns but by individuals, thinkers and entrepreneurs who have a product and the willingness to learn. The best part is, you don't have to go it alone like those early DRTV pioneers.

Over the past few years, companies like ours, Harvest Growth, have been developed to help inventors and entrepreneurs wade through the sea of complexity to make sure their product launches go smoothly.

- **Which vendors do I work with?**
- **How much money do I need to get started?**
- **What should be my creative strategy?**
- **Should I license my product?**

These are all questions that can be answered with the help of an expert in the field.

Parting Words about the History of Infomercials

Two things happened since the early days of pioneering infomercial programming:

1.) **First, it has become easier for the everyday inventor to produce an infomercial and get it on the air.** Technology, creativity and social media are your new best friends! With

Google TV, many can shoot an infomercial with a home HD video camera and literally upload their spot over the Internet without ever having to speak to someone or, for that matter, leave the couch.

2.) **Second, the space has become more crowded as hundreds of new infomercials are tested each month.** It has become more difficult to stand out among the slew of new products. This is why it's important to work with professionals that know the industry and can give your product the best chance for success.

24 hours a day, 7 days a week, millions of dollars are being earned by the direct-response television industry… on a daily basis. If you truly do want to *Sell On TV*, there has never been a better time.

So, what are you waiting for?!?

Chapter 14

Example Financial Projections for a Successful Launch

What will "success" look like for your DRTV product? While money, fame and accolades may sound nice, it's impossible to define success if we can't measure it. And when it comes to finance, we use projections to help us understand what makes a success—or a failure. That's where **Chapter 14**: *Example Financial Projections for a Successful Launch* comes in!

Now we come to the "meat and potatoes" of planning the financials around your hot new creation! Before you invest in taking your product to market, there are a couple of key metrics that you'll want to know:

- **4x to 5x multiple from product cost to retail/TV offer price ($4 cost for a $19.99 is a 5x multiple, $5 is a 4x multiple).** The higher your multiple, the more flexibility you'll have to fund your campaign as your business grows. If your margin is too small, then you won't be able to afford to market your product.

- **60 percent gross margin.** For the DRTV side of the business, the gross margin includes the cost and revenue for all upsells, shipping and handling and all third-party backend costs such as telemarketing, website transaction fees, shipping and fulfillment, returns and credit card processing. For the retail side of the business, your gross margin includes logistics costs, selling, general and administrative costs and other direct product-related costs. The gross margin for both DRTV and retail excludes advertising expenditures, and if your margin falls below 60 percent, it will become very difficult to sufficiently support your business with the necessary advertising and promotion.

The Media Efficiency Ratio, or MER

The Media Efficiency Ratio (MER) is perhaps the most important and most commonly discussed metric in DRTV. It's also just referred to as the "ratio." To arrive at this critical figure, divide your campaign revenue by your media spend. In other words, $20,000 in revenue off of a $10,000 media spend is a 2.0 ratio.

Decision points from MER results:

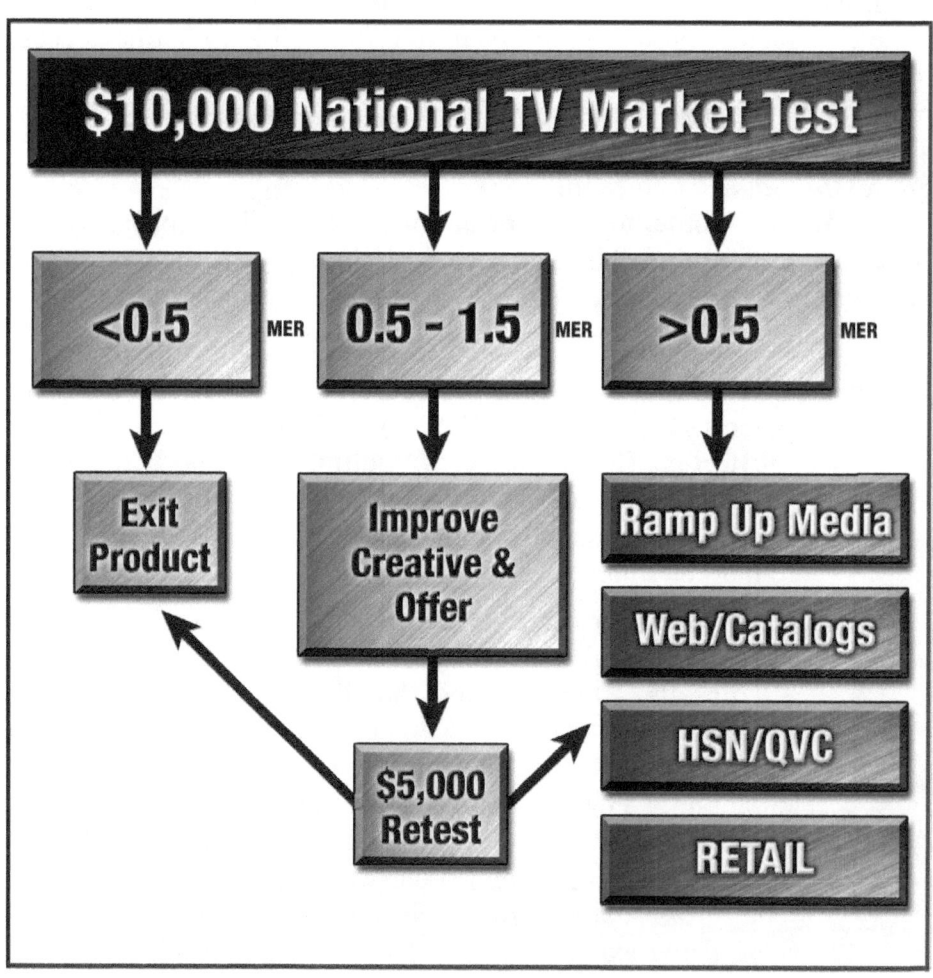

CPO, CPC & RPO: Terms to Know

Have no idea what I'm talking about yet? Rest easy; you're in good company. But here are some simple terms you should understand in order to test the efficacy of your product launch?

- **CPO = Cost Per Order.** This term represents the media cost divided by the number of orders received.
- **CPC = Cost Per Call.** CPC refers to the media cost divided by the number of calls received.
- **RPO = average Revenue Per** Order. Include product upsells and optimized shipping and handling in the mix to increase your average RPO. The higher the RPO, the fewer orders you need to generate in order to be profitable. A high RPO can turn a dead campaign into a winner.

Using the information above, here is an example of how to calculate your break even MER:

OFFER

	Price	S & H Price	% Conversion
Main Offer	$19.99	$6.95	100%
"Get One Free" just pay S & H		$6.95	75%
Upsell 1	$14.99	$6.95	20%
Upsell 2	$14.99	–	20%
Upsell 3	$9.99	–	20%
Upsell 4	$14.99	$6.95	20%
Rush Shipping		$9.95	20%
		Average Sale Price:	**$47.91**

COSTS

	Cost	% Conversion
Telemarketing + Fulfillment	$8.00	
Main Offer	$4.00	100%
"Get One Free" just pay S & H	$4.00	75%
Upsell 1	$3.00	20%
Upsell 2	$3.00	20%
Upsell 3	$3.00	20%
Upsell 4	$3.00	20%
Rush Shipping	$2.00	20%
Total Costs:	**$17.61**	
Margin:	**63.3%**	
Target Margin:	**>60%**	
Breakeven Media Efficiency Ration (MER):	**1.58**	

Ideally, you will want to target a gross margin above 60 percent. The inverse of the gross margin is your breakeven MER. In this example, you need to earn $15,800 in revenue for every $10,000 spent on media (for a 1.58 MER).

Parting Words about Financial Projections for a Successful Launch

When your media is profitable, you can generally double your media spend week over week as you ramp up for the first few weeks and then carefully grow your weekly media after that point to make sure that your campaign remains profitable as you test new networks and day parts (times of day your media runs).

A typical rollout might look like this:

- **Week 1:** $10,000
- **Week 2:** *$20,000*
- **Week 3:** *$40,000*
- **Week 4:** *$65,000*
- **Week 5:** *$100,000*
- **Week 6:** *$150,000*
- **Week 7:** *$200,000*
- **Week 8:** *$250,000*

Chapter 15

Does the Snuggie Come in Yellow? (And Other Frequently Asked Questions)

Do you often wonder how the Snuggie colors were selected?

Or who, exactly, buys all these crazy "As Seen On TV" products?

Or even how quickly you can get your own product to market via DRTV?

Rest easy; now that you know everything you ever wanted to know about how to *Sell On TV* (and a whole lot more!), here's everything *else* you wanted to know about DRTV, but were afraid to ask:

How did they choose those colors for the Snuggie?

People often joke about the "cheesiness" of all those "As Seen On TV" products, but many don't realize that serious market research has gone into the development of each and every product. Unlike at Kraft or Procter & Gamble, where hundreds of thousands of dollars can be spent just on refining a concept, in DRTV, the launch actually becomes the test.

Oftentimes, marketers will test different colors, price points, premiums, product features and creative strategies and roll out the version with the highest ROI. Because DRTV is so results focused, the launch becomes the perfect market research—consumers are telling us what they want not by answering surveys but by pulling out their credit cards and actually ordering.

In many ways, a DRTV launch is like a focus group—with perfectly predictable and scalable results. The fact is, YOU may not rush out to buy a camouflage Snuggie or Chia Pet shaped like Homer Simpson's head, but the fact that it exists and is chewing through so much air time proves that many, many people will—and actively do.

Who buys all this stuff on TV?

The *average* DRTV consumer is older, female and middle-income. That said, As Seen On TV products are purchased by all demographics, by men and women, by old and young, by rich and poor. So while you may have never purchased a product off of TV personally, chances are your next door neighbor has—or your cubicle mate, or the girl who sold you coffee this morning or delivered your pizza last night.

Many consumers wait to see the product in retail, which is why the real profit potential of a given product is realized in retail, but millions can still be made on TV *before a product ever makes it to retail*.

Why do I need a "media test" if you believe in my product?

Though there are several factors that improve your odds of success, no one can predict whether your product will be a home run or not until a media test is performed. You wouldn't think of putting on a Broadway play after just one rehearsal, would you? Media tests are like dress rehearsals; we use them to "work out the kinks" and make sure a product launch is ready to go before it launches.

Case in point: we once worked with an infomercial producer that had developed a process that helped them to claim a "100 percent success rate" for product launches. We cautioned our client against believing this wild claim, but apparently it was too tempting to pass up. No surprise here, the spot this "100 percent success rate" company produced was a complete bomb.

In fact, this client, a DRTV veteran that has dozens of multi-million dollar home runs under their belt in their 25+ year tenure in DRTV, said that this product launch, and I quote, had "the worst results they had seen in many years." Interestingly, the producer maintains the "100 percent success rate" claim on their website.

If the claims are too good to be true, then they most likely aren't true! Claims, hype and phony stats are far less reliable than proven results. The only way to accurately predict the success of a product is *to take it to market.* Spend $10,000 or more in national television media, and see how the results turn out. If they predict a home run, only then will you know that you actually have a home run on your hands.

What happens if the media test is successful, but I don't have the money to ramp up the media spend to turn it into a true "home run?"

There are two types of financial planning: saving and investing. What's the difference? Well, when you save, you merely put money aside for a rainy day. (Nothing wrong with that!) When you invest, however, you roll that money back into increasing profits for you and your family.

Much like investing, profitable advertising leads to more profitable advertising. In other words, when your advertising is profitable, you can take the profits each media week and reinvest them to grow your media spend. However, you may be limited in your resources as to how quickly you can ramp up your media spend and purchase container loads of inventory from China.

One option is to contact a respected media funding company (see recommended vendors on our website, www.SellOnTVBook.com) that will lend you money each week based on the results of your campaign.

Another option is to license your product to a proven DRTV marketing company. As discussed in the licensing chapter, you will keep less from each sale, but you may be able to sell 10 to 100 times as much of your product and *make more money overall.* We're specifically familiar with one example where the inventor has netted almost $10 million in royalties by licensing her product rather than handling it herself.

How long can I expect my product to remain profitable?

The average life-span of the direct-response portion of a campaign in its original format is 6 months to 2 years. However, if the product has retail legs, results can continue for several more years, especially if you are able to successfully build a brand behind your product (for example, OxiClean). Some campaigns can extend their DRTV lifespan through changes to the creative and the offer (Proactiv, for example).

Do I need celebrity talent for my infomercial?

Celebrity hosts are not necessary for every campaign. They become much more important for products in highly competitive categories such as beauty and fitness, but you can generally test your product without celebrity talent and then incur the expense as your campaign grows in order to further improve your profitability.

Think of the Snuggie, Bumpits and many of the other DRTV examples we've used throughout this book and you'll find that the majority of DRTV products are sold without a celebrity talent for their infomercial.

How quickly can I get my product to market via DRTV?

If you are producing a short-form, two-minute spot, you can generally be on national television within 6 to 8 weeks after signing a contract with a producer, assuming you have inventory ready to go. For thirty-minute infomercials, the advertising production timeline is at least twice that, generally 3 months to 5 months after contract signing.

How much does it cost to produce an infomercial?

This is a difficult question to answer in an FAQs section. (In fact, I could write a whole other book about this topic!) Why is it so difficult? Well, for starters, there are a lot of factors that drive the cost of advertising production. Generally speaking, a two-minute spot will cost between $25,000 and $80,000 to produce, and a thirty-minute infomercial will cost anywhere from $100,000 to $1,000,000.

The primary cost drivers are the location of the shooting, host talent, hosted spot vs. voiceover only, green screen vs. location shooting, 3D animation needs and the producer you choose. So you can see how all of these factors, or even one or two, might mean the difference between a $30,000 two-minute spot and one that costs, potentially, twice that much—if not more.

Keep in mind that, in the DRTV industry at least, more expensive doesn't always mean better. Oftentimes, the best producers will produce an infomercial or DRTV spot inexpensively if they believe in your product and you are negotiate backend royalties.

How much of my product can I really sell at 2 in the morning?

First of all, it is a common misconception that infomercials only air in the middle of the night. In fact, short-form, two-minute DRTV spots air on almost every cable station and can air any time of day, from morning to primetime to overnight.

Secondly, does it really matter when you're on TV if you're generating millions of dollars as a result? Sometimes, the best media results *will* come at 2 in the morning. When that's the case, by all means, AIR YOUR SPOT AT 2 A.M. and then LAUGH ALL THE WAY TO THE BANK!

For most products, your spot will air at various times of day on various different networks. It may be successful in the morning on news stations, during primetime on women's networks and at 2 in the morning on music video channels. The beauty of direct response is that you will know when is the most profitable time to air your spot on each station, unlike expensive retail advertising that will "guess" at when the most profitable time is and may miss out on millions of dollars of profit by taking this "gamble" with your precious airtime.

For long-form, thirty-minute infomercials, you are a bit more restricted in your media selection. After all, that's as long as most sitcom or Family Guy episodes, so you can kiss primetime goodbye. Overnight and Saturday morning media are very common for major cable and network stations, but there are a few stations that air infomercials 24 hours per day.

Since media buys are so important, it can be helpful—even prudent—to find a trusted media buyer to help guide you through this process.

Which is better: live operator telemarketers or Interactive Voice Response (IVR)?

Interactive Voice Response, or IVR, has only been around for a few short years in the DRTV industry, and many of the major DRTV marketers were originally hesitant to try out the new technology.

How does IVR work? Basically, a script is recorded and callers either say their responses to questions or press the keypad on their telephone. Today, nearly all $10 to $19.99 products are sold via IVR. The cost is significantly lower per minute, and surprisingly, the order conversion results are generally higher. It's generally a no-brainer to use IVR for less expensive products.

As your price point increases, so does the likelihood that live operators will work better for your campaign. Higher ticket items generally take more convincing to convert a call into a sale. As do complex offers like free trials, continuity programs, soft offers (where the price isn't mentioned in the creative, such as with products like Bowflex, for instance) and multiple payment offers. In these instances, live operators can significantly increase your conversion.

As with most recommendations in this industry, your gut may not always be right. Many inventors think that their product needs live operators so it doesn't seem so "infomercially." However, bottom line profitability is what you should focus on, not just image. What's more, the IVR technology has come so far in the past few years that it's actually a pretty smooth, and sometimes preferred, experience for callers.

So, how do I get started?

We're glad you (finally) asked! Review our industry resources on this book's website: www.SellOnTVBook.com and start calling vendors, or hire a DRTV marketing consultant to walk you through the process. Selling millions of your product on TV and in retail can happen in just a few short months, so what are you waiting for?

Chapter 16

Industry Resources—The Best of the Best

Selling on TV and, eventually, in retail is not done in a vacuum. Networks and connections must exist to ensure that our product reaches the masses. How is that done? With lots and lots of providers.

Over the years, we have worked with all the top providers in the industry. They each have their strengths and weaknesses, and some are better for certain types of products and campaigns than others. You can contact each of them and negotiate rates on your own, or feel free to call our Harvest Growth office to ask advice on which vendors are best for your product launch.

We've also seen clients try to select unproven vendors and fall flat on their face. If you do everything right with your DRTV marketing campaign but work with the wrong telemarketing, website or media buyer vendor, your home run campaign can look like a strike out in fewer than three swings! There is too much at risk to take chances. Work with proven resources to give your product the best chances of being a home run.

Visit our website, www.SellOnTVBook.com for detailed contact information for each of the following vendor categories. Because companies can come and go, we maintain an actively updated list on our website rather than publishing them in a static book that may contain inaccurate information if a company changes its phone number or website, for instance:

Telemarketing

While you may not enjoy getting their calls at dinnertime, when it comes to DRTV, telemarketing can either make or break an otherwise flawless launch. Often the unseen heroes of the DRTV, telemarketing call centers, both live operators and IVR systems, are on the front lines when your customer calls the 1-800 number provided on the air.

Generally speaking, 50 percent to 70 percent of your sales will come via telephone orders, so this vendor selection is especially crucial to the success of your product launch. Luckily, there are several vendors that have great track records converting calls to sales.

Website Development

It might seem like a website would be the least of your DRTV problems, but in fact a poor, simplistic or unsophisticated website can really damage a product launch. You *can* develop your own website, but there are several vendors in the DRTV industry that cost less than $5,000 and have a history of producing high-converting websites with high average orders. Even the largest DRTV marketers generally use these outside agencies to develop their products' websites due to the low cost and high value added.

A good DRTV website developer can turn a losing campaign into a winner. DRTV website developers are also connected to vast affiliate networks and are able to add 20 percent to 30 percent to your top line revenues through email campaigns, banner campaigns and affiliate sales.

Fulfillment

Whatever you do with this list of resources, we implore you: *please choose a proven DRTV fulfillment center*. This is the vendor that is most often overlooked by inventors and entrepreneurs new to DRTV. And we understand why; it seems so easy. All they have to do is pack and ship the product, right?

It seems like you could do that yourself, doesn't it? But, in fact, this is one of the most sophisticated and challenging steps of the process. Everything can go right with your launch but if customers can't get the product, everything will go wrong from there.

If you have a buddy that owns a fulfillment center, he'll promise you great cost savings and tell you that although he's never worked in DRTV before, it's an easy transition. Not true! The manner in which orders are collected by telemarketers and DRTV websites means that the credit cards are not processed at the time of orders, and this tends to gum up the process with inexperienced fulfillment centers.

We once worked with a $100 million fulfillment operation that was new to DRTV. What seemed so "easy" to them at the start proved a nightmare for our client, who ended up losing several thousand dollars in lost customers, extra processing fees and eventual transition costs to a new, proven DRTV fulfillment center.

Don't experiment with processing and fulfillment; find a proven vendor who isn't doing this for the first time. This is NOT the time to be a buddy's, a friend's or heaven forbid a family member's "guinea pig."

Media Buying

There are literally dozens of DRTV media buyers, and the more vendors you contact, the better each deal seems. One may charge a 15 percent commission and another a 5 percent media commission. Seems like an obvious choice, right?

Not so fast: *you can't forget media rates*. The best media buyers generally charge higher commissions, upwards of 15 percent, but their negotiated remnant media rates with the cable networks can be as much as 50 percent lower than smaller vendors. Choose wisely.

Credit Card Payment Processing

With hundreds of credit card processors to choose from, it's a daunting task to choose the right one for your campaign. With the huge spikes in volumes you can see in DRTV, you need to work with a vendor that won't get scared off by big jumps in volume and cut you off. (And don't think it hasn't happened; it has!)

It is a nightmare often experienced by new vendors: jump from $10,000 in sales to $200,000 in a month's time. Sounds like a dream come true, right? Well, it can quickly turn into a nightmare when your card company holds all your revenue for several months refusing to deposit into your account.

In the meantime, a competitor can step in and steal your market. The best vendors are working with dozens of DRTV clients at a time, and they simply don't cut off your revenues because they understand the industry. For a comprehensive listing of our recommended credit card processors, visit our website, www.SellOnTVBook.com for detailed contact information.

Advertising Production

Not all advertising production companies are created equal. Some producers specialize in short form; some in long form. Many are generalists, while others specialize in certain product categories. The vast majority of producers work only "part time" in the DRTV industry, choosing to fill their remaining time with other advertising and television production.

Go with a specialist. We recommend you choose an advertising producer that focuses *100 percent on DRTV*. They will best know the ins and outs of DRTV and have more incentive to make your product work because this IS their day job and not just another sideline or "freelance" gig. Instead, they live or die on the success of their campaigns rather than staying afloat through other means.

Media Funding

If you have a successful campaign and limited funds, these vendors can fund your media to help you grow your campaign extremely quickly. First-time inventors to $300mm DRTV marketers alike commonly use these vendors.

Product Licensing

If you have a proven campaign but lack the resources or the interest to ramp up quickly, you can always license to a proven marketer to maximize your product revenues (and royalties in your pocket) very quickly. Again, it all comes down to results; these deals are easy to come by once your product is proven in market.

International Distribution

Are you hesitant about moving into foreign markets? Are you unwilling, or unable, to adopt the "global marketplace" theory? True enough, the U.S. market is huge. You can literally generate hundreds of millions of dollars without ever crossing the fiscal border. However, you could be leaving significant profits on the table by staying 100 percent focused on the U.S. market.

Case in point: OxiClean waited too long to enter the European market, and Reckitt Benckiser launched copycat products all over Europe before OxiClean "crossed the pond." By the time OxiClean made it to Europe, they were a distant second, constantly fighting for market position despite their undisputed dominance in the domestic marketplace. They never experienced a similar level of success in Europe, and today OxiClean is difficult to find on European store shelves.

What a lost opportunity!

You don't need to set up an office for your company abroad to capture those markets. There are several proven distributors that can do all the legwork to get you into Europe, Asia, South America... even Mexico and Canada. Some of them will even do all the repackaging into different languages at their own expense, and may even redub your infomercial into different languages and pay for the media.

If it's out of your comfort zone, that's okay; it's worth it! This can generate millions to your bottom line with minimal effort on your part, allowing you to focus on the vast U.S. market while still reaping the profits from abroad.

Retail Sales Brokers

Even $300 million brands like OxiClean are often sold into mass retailers through brokers and outside sales reps rather than through internal reps. Brokers and reps live in the same neighborhoods as the retail buyers. It's an insider, locals-only clannish affair and that definitely works in your favor. These guys and gals frequently go to lunch together and coach each others' kids' little league teams. They have relationships that would take you years to try and replicate; don't even try!

Many do not charge monthly fees, so you only pay on successful sales into mass retailers. It's worth the expense to hire proven sales reps to do a lot of the legwork, whether you are a $100,000 emerging brand or a $100 million proven powerhouse.

HSN/QVC Sales Reps

Is HSN and/or QVC part of your overall plan to take over and dominate the airwaves? Then you'll need these guys! Similar to retail brokers, HSN and QVC reps can be an immense help in getting you on to these networks. You may submit your product on your own, and it could take months for the buyer to even see your submission.

Good HSN/QVC reps are in the networks' office every week meeting with the buyers and can get you a quick response. Similar to retail, most of the good brokers are paid on success. If you don't get on the networks, you don't owe a dime.

About the Author

Jon LaClare, CEO, Harvest Growth

My name is Jon LaClare, and I have made a business out of selling on TV. In fact, I live to help new brands emerge and old brands come back to life. Always the entrepreneur-in-training, I have wanted to own my own business and bring exciting products to market since I was a young boy in Cleveland, Ohio. To this day, in fact, my wife laughs at the photo of me walking to kindergarten carrying a briefcase.

Turns out briefcases would be a part of my professional attire for years to come. After graduating with a B.S. in Accounting from Brigham Young University, I started my professional career in public accounting with Ernst & Young in Boston, MA, but quickly realized that my passions were about driving ideas forward rather than focusing on the past.

After two invigorating years at the University of Chicago Graduate School of Business, where I received my MBA, I began an exciting marketing career helping some of the biggest brands in the world bring innovative products to market and grow the bottom line. Some highlights were the category-changing OxiClean Detergent Ball, Kaboom Bowl Blaster and OxiClean Miracle Foam, as well as the indulgent HoneyMaid Soft Baked Snack Bars and kid-friendly Nabisco 100 Calorie Packs.

Today, I realize my dreams through helping inventors, entrepreneurs and growth-minded companies drive their products into what I call "hyper-growth." I do it through a company called Harvest Growth (www.HarvestGrowth.com) that I own with my energetic British business partner Jason Williams in beautiful Colorado. Together, we've launched and managed products that now total over $1Billion in annual sales. When it comes to selling on TV, we've worked with the best of the best, the brightest of the brightest and now we're ready to share our industry secrets with you.

Jon can be reached at:

Harvest Growth LLC
753 Maleta Lane, Ste 204
Castle Rock, CO 80108
(720) 207-9493
jon@harvestgrowth.com
www.harvestgrowth.com

www.ingramcontent.com/pod-product-compliance
Lightning Source LLC
Chambersburg PA
CBHW022101170526
45157CB00004B/1434